A LIGHT in the DARKNESS

Stories About God's Mysterious Ways from GUIDEPOSTS

Arthur Gordon,
Elizabeth Searle Lamb,
and Oth

DIMENSIONS
FOR LIVING
NASHVILLE

A LIGHT IN THE DARKNESS

First Dimensions for Living edition 1996

Copyright © 1993 by Guideposts Associates, Inc., Carmel, NY 10512

All rights reserved. No part of this book may be reproduced, stored in a retrieval system or transmitted in any form or by any means, electronic, mechanical, photocopying, recording or otherwise, except for brief quotations in reviews, without the written permission of the publisher. Address inquiries to Rights & Permissions Department, Guideposts Associates, Inc., 16 E. 34th St., New York, NY 10016.

This book is printed on recycled, acid-free paper.

Library of Congress Cataloging-in-Publication Data

Gordon, Arthur.
A light in the darkness : stories about God's mysterious ways from Guideposts / Arthur Gordon, Elizabeth Searle Lamb, and others.
p.   cm.
ISBN 0-687-00248-6 (alk. paper)
1. Providence and government of God—Case studies.   2. Christian life—Anecdotes.   3. Miracles—Case studies.   I. Lamb, Elizabeth Searle.
II. Title.
BT135.G65   1996
231'.5—dc20
95-46429
CIP

All Scripture quotations, unless otherwise noted, are from the King James or Authorized Version of the Bible.

Scripture quotations marked NRSV are from the New Revised Standard Version Bible, copyright © 1989, by the Division of Christian Education of the National Council of the Churches of Christ in the United States of America. Used by permission.

Scripture quotations marked NIV are taken from the Holy Bible: New International Version. Copyright © 1973, 1978, 1984 by the International Bible Society. Used by permission of Zondervan Bible Publishers.

Every attempt has been made to credit the sources of copyright material used in this book. If any such acknowledgment has been inadvertently omitted or miscredited, receipt of such information would be appreciated.

Except as noted below, and for some poems, all material appeared originally in *Guideposts* magazine. Copyright © 1953, 1959, 1972, 1975, 1976, 1977, 1978, 1980, 1981, 1986, 1988, 1990, 1991, 1992, 1993.

"A Strange Soft Light," by Malcolm Muggeridge is from *Something Beautiful for God*, by Malcolm Muggeridge, copyright © The Mother Teresa Committee, 1971, and is reprinted by permission of HarperCollins.

"A Friend Was in Danger," by Margaret Mackay, is condensed from the book *I Live in a Suitcase*, by Margaret Mackay, published in 1953 by the John Day Co.

The poem "God Fashioned a House," is from Grace Livingston Hill, *The Parkerstown Delegate*.

96 97 98 99 00 01 02 — 10 9 8 7 6 5 4 3 2 1
MANUFACTURED IN THE UNITED STATES OF AMERICA

Grace Hauenstein Library
Aquinas College
Grand Rapids, MI 49506

CONTENTS

3. WHEN WE BELIEVE

4. WHEN WE PRAY

5. WHEN WE SEE CHRIST

PREFACE

My cousin Anna was not—"relatively" speaking—a close cousin, but we were very close. I say this in spite of the fact that in the years after my tenth birthday I lived in New York and she in Kentucky. We only saw each other maybe once a year and neither of us kept in touch with letters. Anna must have been in her late forties by the time I came into my teens, though I never thought much about the difference in our ages. We were friends. Soul mates, you might say.

One night during my junior year of high school I put away my homework, turned out the light, and slipped into bed. But I did not go to sleep. I began to think about Anna. The clock ticked. Sleep would not come. *Anna. Anna.* She simply would not leave my thoughts. Finally I got up out of bed, turned on the light, sat down at the desk and wrote her a letter. She never received it. That was the night Anna died.

Her death shook me, yet shocked and saddened as I was, what really unnerved me was how Anna had come so insistently to mind as I struggled for sleep that night. It made me feel odd. Had I dreamed it all? No, the letter was proof that something real had happened between Anna and me. Even so, it gave me such a strange feeling that I was reluctant to tell anybody about it. Today, however, I no longer try to fathom the mystery of that night. I simply accept it gratefully as a beautiful spiritual confirmation of how close Anna and I were to each other.

Back then I had no way of knowing that other people had similar mystical experiences they couldn't explain. Now, after many years as Editor-in-Chief of Guideposts magazine, I know that these things happen all the time. Again and again readers of the magazine have written to tell us of the strange happenings in their lives. The book you hold in your hands, like its predecessor *Wings in the Wilderness,* is filled with such accounts. As you read them may I suggest that you do as I did and not struggle for explanations. Stand in awe if you will, but be grateful for their mystery. See them as a wonderful confirmation of God's presence in our lives.

VAN VARNER
Editorial Director

ONE

THE SHINING LIGHT

*S*uddenly a light from heaven flashed around him.

—Acts 9:3 NRSV

"God is light," the apostle John tells us (I John 1:5). He is "the Father of lights" according to the apostle James (1:17), the author and giver of good and perfect gifts. So it's no surprise to discover that he uses light and lights to communicate with us. The lights we read about in this section are of three kinds: the light of God's presence; lights mysteriously shining that point to God or that help people in trouble; and the light of love that, though unmeasurable by a light meter, still shows up on film, proving the truth of the psalmist's comment, "In thy light shall we see light" (Psalm 36:9).

WHY WERE OUR LANDING LIGHTS ON?

G. H. Beaulaurier

On a cold January night I was captain of United Airlines flight 840 bound for San Francisco. We had taken off from Denver and had climbed to about twenty-nine thousand feet when a flight attendant knocked at the cockpit door. A passenger, she said, had just reported seeing a light flashing an SOS in the mountains beneath us. I no sooner got a fix on our position—sixty-two miles west of Denver on the J-60 airway—when the intercom chimed and another flight attendant told us of a second passenger who had seen the SOS signal.

Enough said. We called Air Traffic Control, advised them of the reports, and gave the estimated location. A commuter flight scheduled over that area was alerted to watch for the distress signal. The sheriff's office was apprised of the situation.

Not until we landed did we learn the whole story. Two people in a four-wheel drive vehicle had ignored the "road closed due to snow" signs posted by the forest service and were trapped by an avalanche.

For two days and nights, they fought fatigue and frostbite. In desperation, they removed a headlight from the vehicle and rigged it to the battery so that they could send out SOS signals. Then they waited. But all the planes flying overhead were too high for them to see at night—until we came along. And the only reason they were able to spot our jetliner was because our landing lights were on.

Our landing lights? To this day I do not know why those lights were on. Or do I?

SHELTER

Christine Brandenberger

*A*ll day long I had dreaded the thirty-mile drive. As a transplanted Californian, I wasn't used to gray, unpredictable Aprils in Kansas. April 27 had been raw and drizzly, and at four o'clock, when I left to take the children to their cousin Stacey's birthday party, it was raining in earnest.

"Be extra careful," my husband, Bill, cautioned as Jennie, five, and Maria, three and a half, wrestled with their coats. I bundled our three-month-old baby, Will, into a satin sleeper. Bill wasn't coming with us because he needed time to study for upcoming medical-school exams.

The birthday party was worth the drive. My girls were impressed with Stacey's Holly Hobbie cake, and they were delighted to "help" play with Stacey's new doll. But when it was time to start for home, the sky was black and the rain torrential; the radio announced that fifty-mile-an-hour winds were buffeting the area. The dirt roads I'd come on would be nearly impassable, so Bill's father mapped out a route that would keep me on paved ones. I scooted the kids into our rattly '67 Plymouth.

I crept down the highway. I couldn't use my bright lights—the solid sheet of rain reflected them back in my face. With my dims, I could see only a few feet ahead. Somewhere I missed a turn and found myself on a gravel road. I turned at the next intersection, thinking I could backtrack to the highway.

I crept along mile after mile. The highway never appeared. I crossed a bridge—and the bottom seemed to fall out of the road. The car dropped, then bumped, and the wheels spun. I found myself on a dirt access road that curved along farm fields next to the riverbank. I shifted into low gear hoping for enough traction to pull myself out, but the car slipped sideways into a slough of mud. And stuck.

Wanting to save the battery, I switched off the lights and sat in the darkness, trying to calm my panic. The road I'd glimpsed in front of me was little more than a path, and it was highly unlikely anyone would be traveling on it before morning. Worse, the river might overflow if the rain continued. We would be swept away.

Lord, I prayed, *help me get the children out of here.*

The instant I looked up I spotted what appeared to be a yard light.

"There's a house just up the road," I told the girls. "We'll walk up there and call Daddy. I'll have to carry Will, so you both must hold tight to my coat pockets. The road will be filled with puddles, so whatever happens, don't let go."

The rain subsided to a drizzle just as we got out of the car. I was thankful for that, but the road was slick and uneven and we kept losing our footing. Worse, we'd only walked a few yards when, to my bewilderment, I realized the yard light I'd seen from the car had disappeared. I couldn't see anything at all.

The girls were afraid, and so was I! To reassure us, we sang "Jesus Loves Me" over and over again. But then Jennie stopped singing.

"If Jesus loves us, why isn't he down here with us?" she asked.

"Honey, it isn't Jesus' fault that Mommy got lost and stuck," I told her. "But Jesus really is with us, and he's showing me the way to go."

But why isn't Jesus *walking* with us?" Jennie persisted.

All I could think of to say was, "He doesn't want to get his feet muddy."

Jennie and Maria giggled, but my fear was only relieved for a moment. Will was heavy—thirteen pounds—and my arms felt ready to drop off. The girls were dragging on my coat pockets, and I knew we couldn't go much farther.

A huge bolt of lightning split the sky, then hung suspended for several seconds, revealing a two-story white farmhouse. If the lightning had flashed twenty seconds later, we might have missed it completely.

We slogged our way onto the front porch, and I knocked on the door, first firmly, then more and more frantically. But the house was dark inside and no one answered. In desperation I tried the knob. Locked.

I sat the girls down on the steps and put Will in Jennie's arms.

"I'm going to the back door," I said. "The people who live here must be in bed, but I'm sure they'll wake up and let us in."

The back door was locked too. I beat on it until my hands hurt. I yelled until I was hoarse. No one came.

The rain started again, an incredible downpour, and the wind whipped it into a stinging frenzy. My children waited unprotected in the chilling gale.

Break into someone's home? *Never.* But I *had* to get into that house.

"Mommy!" Jennie screamed from the front porch. I could hear Maria crying.

I took a deep breath, doubled my fist and smashed it through the pane of glass alongside the back door. I reached in, pulled back the bolt, and flung the door open. Then I ran back around to the front, swept up the children and rushed them through the back door.

We held on to one another breathlessly, then looked around. An old floor lamp shone with just enough dim light for me to see the outlines of a stove . . . a refrigerator . . . And . . . a telephone! Help was only a phone call away! I hurried to it.

The line was dead.

I put back the receiver and sank wearily against the wall. Will started to whimper. I flipped a light switch. Nothing. I tried another, then another. Nothing. Yet for some reason the single bulb of that dilapidated floor lamp gave forth a pale but steady light. Without it, we'd have been in total darkness.

The house didn't have much furniture, but there was a worn sofa covered in houndstooth-check nylon. I used the cushions to make a bed on the floor for the girls. When I pulled off their muddy slacks, I saw that Maria had walked right out of her little T-strap shoes somewhere on the muddy road and had continued barefoot. But she and Jennie had obeyed my instructions to hold on: My coat pockets were nearly ripped off.

"Mommy, are we safe now?" Jennie asked tiredly.

"Of course we are, darling," I said. Thank goodness she and her sister were too tired to detect the quiver of uneasiness in my voice. I was feeling anything but safe.

We had found shelter, but was that enough? True, there was a roof over our heads, and walls between us and the stormy blast. But my heart still beat anxiously. I had broken into the home of people I didn't know, damaged their property and used their possessions without permission. The walls around us kept out the wind and the rain, but my heart still beat uneasily. I was cold and feeling like the intruder I was.

A lightning flash illuminated the room, and my eyes fell on a small wooden plaque on a built-in hutch. I picked up the plaque and carried it to the kitchen lamp, where I read these words written in white:

THE LORD IS MY SHEPHERD.

A sense of peace enfolded me like two loving arms. This was a house where God-fearing people lived. And God was here. Now.

I lay down with my arms around the children, watching the play of lightning and listening to the wind, rain, and thunder. I was still worried about Bill and his parents. What would they think had happened to us? But I felt calm and secure for the first time in hours.

It must have been about 1:30 in the morning when I heard the click of a key in the front lock. I jumped up and hurried to the door and came face-to-face with a young man who looked as surprised as I was.

I poured out my story of why I was there, explaining that I'd never have broken in if I hadn't been desperate. "And," I ended breathlessly, "I knew, whoever you were, you'd be nice."

"Lady," he said, "I'm the owner of this house, and I hoped, whoever *you* were, that you'd be nice too."

The young man lived with his parents in town but was fixing up the house to live in after his upcoming marriage. He worked the late shift at a nearby plant, and on his way home had felt a strong urge to come by the house to see if the storm had done any damage.

He helped me carry the children to his car and took us to his parents' home, where I called my family. They had been frantically driving all over the countryside looking for us.

The next day, we returned to pay him for the damages and give him a plant as a small token of our thanks. He towed our car out with a tractor, and he even found little Maria's shoes in the mud. By that time his electricity, which had been knocked out by the storm, had been restored. He had no idea what yard light we could have seen, or why the dim kitchen light had continued to glow.

But he did know why the plaque was there. "Well, sure," he said matter-of-factly. "I put it there."

The Lord is my shepherd.

The young man's home was not just a shelter for us; it was a sanctuary.

THE LIGHT AND THE CROSS

Arthur Gordon

*I*n an airliner I found myself sitting next to a young woman who told me that she was a registered nurse. When she learned that I was a writer, she said, "I'll tell you a story, a true one. Maybe you can use it."

I smiled a little. "Maybe I can."

"Last week," she said, "I was on night duty. The patient in room seventy-eight was very frightened. Surgery was scheduled for the next morning and I knew the doctors did not give this woman much of a chance.

"I tried to cheer her and suggested that she pray for strength. She said she did not believe that prayers were answered, but I urged her to pray anyway.

"During the night I went into her darkened room with my flashlight to see if she was all right. Then, rather suddenly, I was called away.

"In the morning a most extraordinary change had come over her. She no longer seemed frightened. 'I'm going to be all right,' she told me. 'I know, because I prayed, and my prayers were answered. I asked for a sign, and I was given one.'

"A sign?

" 'I saw a light,' she said in a whisper. 'And in the center of the light, a cross. It was on the wall at the foot of my bed. I'm going to be all right.'

"The attendants came then, and wheeled her away. When she was gone, I looked in the blankets at the foot of her bed and found what I was looking for—my flashlight. A week or so earlier I had dropped it, had cracked the glass, and had mended it with a tiny cross of adhesive tape. Obviously, when I came in during the night, I had left it by mistake. Half-buried in the blankets, it must have projected a circle of light, just as the patient said . . . with a cross in the center."

"And did the patient recover?"

"Of course she did! She thought her prayers were answered."

The nurse's voice died away. For a moment there was nothing but the drone of the engines.

"And what do you think?" I asked her.

The nurse smiled and shook her head. "I don't think," she said. "I know!"

A LIGHT IN THE DARKNESS

Dicky Roth

*T*he rain crashed like clouds of bullets on the cobbled streets of Oslo. Yet steadily more people joined the ranks, until they were eight-deep on each side of the road. And they were smiling.

"What's taking place?" I asked a man.

"It's Haakon's birthday," he said. "He'll ride through Oslo at two o'clock."

It was only noon, yet there they stood, surely every one of Oslo's four hundred thousand, in the heavy deluge.

It was 1952, and I was making a colored film of Norway. The procession obviously would provide some fine shots. But in the rain there was barely enough light to see, let alone for color photography.

And yet I sensed a strange glow all around me. A soft light seemed to fill the streets. I searched everywhere but could not find its source. Puzzled, I took out my light-meter and measured the light; it registered nil. Still I knew there was a light, coming from somewhere.

Then, quite foolishly for a professional photographer

who should know better, I reached for my camera and started filming.

At last, at long wet last, the procession came out—one ordinary, everyday *open* car, one motorcycle cop at each side, a sound-car behind. That was all!

In the backseat of the open car an elderly man sat alone. As he approached, an immense sound arose from the people.

It started as a mighty cheer, then seemed to stumble: four hundred thousand lumps in four hundred thousand throats. One got into mine, too, as I looked at that kindly figure, erect and smiling, with the rain beating him mercilessly.

I ground my camera and then dashed ahead in my car. I reached the big hospital ahead of the procession and there, to my horror, on the pavement in the pouring rain, in beds, wheelchairs, stretchers, I found the sick, the lame, the halt—umbrellas held over them, carefully covered up with hospital rubber sheeting, nurses and doctors standing behind them—all smiling radiantly.

I cried out, impulsively, "Oh, dear people, you mustn't wait out here! There's nothing to see. There's only one car with one man in it."

They all looked at me compassionately, their bright smiles never leaving their rain-spattered faces. Then one man spoke:

"Thank you," he said in English, "but, you see, that one man is Haakon, today is his eightieth birthday. And it is not only that we want to see *him*, we want *him* to see *us*. Each of us wants Haakon to know that today we wish him well."

As I listened to him other things I'd heard came back to me. . . . The tailor, fitting my new coat, who had chatted of the Oslo Rotary Club where the King drops in informally. "Haakon is the head both of our government and our Norwegian Lutheran Church. He likes to know about all of our problems . . ." The bus driver who talked about the German invasion and Haakon's refusal to replace the Norwegian cabinet with Nazi-picked men. Escaping the German purge, Haakon removed his government to England where he kept up the fight. I remembered, too, that Norwegians never say "The day the war ended," but "The day Haakon came home . . ."

Just then the car with Haakon in it drove past. Up went the most robust cheer I ever heard—from wheelchairs, beds, and stretchers. He waved to them and was gone. The cheer quieted into a collective, tender sigh.

When, at 6:30 that evening in the pouring rain, Haakon spoke from the balcony of the Town Hall, I was there with my camera. And as the crowds still danced in the streets at eleven o'clock, I was still, idiotically, filming in the dark.

Next day I stacked up all the film I'd used and wasted. Weeks later, when they came back to me, processed, I tossed them aside without troubling to examine them. I knew they would be blank.

But one day, tidying up my workshop before throwing the whole pack out, I half-heartedly put one roll of "Haakon's Birthday" on the projector. I gasped! It had all come out—in color!

Stunned, I reran the film, again and again. Everything I had photographed was there: the rain, the people, Haakon. Despite the dark day, the scenes were vividly clear and colorful. Suddenly, I discovered where the precious light originated. It was in the people's eyes as they looked fondly at their leader—the man whose own devout goodness and dedication had aroused in them a deep devotion. Studying their faces on the screen, I realized that on a dark day in Oslo I had filmed King Haakon's birthday procession by the light of pure *love*!

Love

William Blake

from The Clod and the Pebble

Love seeketh not itself to please,
Nor for itself hath any care,
But for another gives its ease,
And builds a Heaven in Hell's despair.

A STRANGE SOFT LIGHT

Malcolm Muggeridge

*A*fter the experience of interviewing Mother Teresa, I had a consuming desire to go to Calcutta and participate in making a television program about her and her work. This became possible in the spring of 1969, thanks to the British Broadcasting Company. Our cameraman was Ken Macmillan, who covered himself with glory filming the Kenneth Clark series, *Civilization*.

We arrived at Calcutta airport on one of those heavy, humid days for which Bengal is famous. The air seems to distill into water as one breathes it, and every movement costs one a stupendous effort. A general strike, we were told, had been organized for the following day. As we only had five days to do our filming, we decided to go almost at once to 54A Lower Circular Road, the address of the Missionaries of Charity. Mother Teresa was waiting for us in the little courtyard of their house. The sight of her, or even the thought of her, always gives me a great feeling of happiness.

The filming began. It is not just my opinion, but that of all concerned, that it proceeded with quite exceptional smoothness and speed; our next move always seemed to be obvious; there were none of the usual breakdowns and crises. Above all, there was no bickering or quarreling, which, in the circumstances of filmmaking, is almost unavoidable. In the ordinary way, making a fifty-minute documentary, which is what our film came out at, takes two to three months. To produce a sufficiency of footage in five days necessarily put a heavy strain on all concerned; it was impossible to get a report on the film taken before moving elsewhere, so there was no chance of redoing any that was unsatisfactory. As it turned out, all was well.

All this amounted to a kind of miracle. There was another actual miracle. Part of the work of the sisters is to pick up the dying from the streets and bring them into a building given to Mother Teresa (a sometime temple dedicated to the cult of the goddess Kali), there, as she puts it, to die within sight of a loving face. Some do die; others survive and are cared for.

This Home for the Dying is dimly lit by small, high windows, and Ken was adamant that filming was quite impossible there. We could not get the place adequately lighted in the time at our disposal. It was decided that, nonetheless, Ken should have a go, but by way of insurance he took, as well, some film in an outside court-yard.

In the processed film, the part taken inside was bathed in a particularly beautiful soft light, whereas the part taken outside was rather dim and confused.

How to account for this? Ken has all along insisted that, technically speaking, the result is impossible. To prove the point, he used some of the same stock in a similarly poor light, with completely negative results. I am absolutely convinced that the technically unac-countable light is, in fact, the "Kindly Light" Newman refers to in his well-known exquisite hymn.

Mother Teresa's Home for the Dying is overflowing with love, as one senses immediately on entering it. This love is luminous, like the halos artists have seen and made visible round the heads of the saints. I find it not at all surprising that the luminosity should register on a photographic film. The supernatural is only an infi-nite projection of the natural, as the furthest horizon is an image of eternity.

One thing everyone who has seen the film seems to be agreed about is that the light in the Home for the Dying is quite exceptionally lovely. This is, from every point of view, highly appropriate. Dying derelicts from the streets might normally be supposed to be some-what repellent, giving off stenches, emitting strange groans. Actually, if the Home for the Dying were piled high with flowers and resounding with musical chants—as it may well have been in its Kali days—it could not be more restful and serene. So the light con-veys perfectly what the place is really like: an outward and visible luminosity manifesting God's inward and invisible present love. This is precisely what miracles are for—to reveal the inner reality of God's outward creation.

A FRIEND WAS IN DANGER

Margaret Mackay

After World War II, I made a close friend in Alicia, an American living in London, who had been a very brave Red Cross girl in the Pacific. On a volunteer job in the tropics, she had picked up one of those grim diseases that are slow in developing. She had married, with outstanding happiness, before she found that the germ was insidiously eating away her strength.

Then she put up a heroic fight to keep her marriage and her home going. When the doctors said that most other people would have been dead, she set out to regain her health, by courage—and by faith. She stayed up most of the time, dragging about gamely, but every now and then she would have a spell that would keep her in bed for weeks, in pain and fever and attrition.

Oddly enough, wherever I might be, and even though we might not write to each other for weeks, I always seemed to feel it in my bones when she was having one of her attacks. Then I would send her a cheerful letter by special delivery, or a light, irrelevant telegram.

One November day I was down in Italy when I sensed—out of nowhere, like an odor—that she was very ill indeed. I sent off a nonchalant telegram about missing her in Rome and hoping to see her at Christmas time. Then, though I had no answer, I wrote every two or three days for several weeks. I carried the sensation of her need with me like a drop of cologne on my hand-kerchief, so that I was poignantly aware of her wherever I went.

I do not happen to be a Catholic, but I love to go into the old Roman churches with their rich residue of the countless prayers that have gone up like incense, and the contact with the innumerable people who have said them in sorrow and hope and gratitude. During those weeks, I often lit a candle and put a few lire in the box for the poor, and also for Alicia.

In Italian towns there are little shrines on many street corners: majolica plaques built into the masonry above the cobblestones, with a lamp flickering; or painted and lighted figures of the Madonna and Child. And wherever I saw these—hundreds of them, as I returned northward through Italy and up into Switzerland—I would pause and think a prayer for Alicia.

In Switzerland, my bedroom window looked out into an Alpine snow scene, with white-frosted fir trees and the spire of a small Gothic church. Above the church door, in a niche curtained with hanging snow, was a miniature shrine, with a stone-carved Madonna, simple and touching as a country doll. A little lamp was kept burning underneath.

Whenever I went to the window, there was the shrine; and there, for me, was Alicia. One night I could not sleep. I got out of bed and crept shivering to the window. In the snowy stillness, with not even a star in the hushed dark, the tiny lamp was burning steadily. I put all my heart into the thought of it then, for I sensed somehow that Alicia had reached her crisis.

And as it turned out—she had. A few days later, I had a note from her husband, telling me that she had been very ill for weeks and was just starting to recover from the worst attack of all.

When I got back to London before the holidays, I found her pale and bony, but nevertheless up on her feet and struggling to make a vivid Christmas for her Charlie—who adored her, as well he might.

"I was really very critically ill this time," she told me, while we sat on a sofa before the fire. "Charlie says I was delirious. He says I kept babbling about a little shrine. And one night, when my fever was very high, and I was in desperate pain—I can't recall anything else out of the blur of misery, but one thing stays with me distinctly. I can remember seeing a dark scene, and a tiny lamp burning, and—clear as if it were right before my eyes—a Madonna and Child in a little shrine."

SEEING THE LIGHT

Virginia Sendor

Some years ago a chain of deaths—my mother's, a younger brother's, a close aunt's—left me utterly grief-stricken and despairing. If only I had used my time with Mama more wisely during her last days! Did she and Richard and Aunt Julia ever known how much I really loved them? Was there anything they had wanted to tell me before they died, but I never gave them a chance?

Despite my professional background in rehabilitation

counseling, I was haunted by painful feelings and questions. I decided to enroll in a graduate workshop on "Counseling for Death, Dying, and Bereavement" at Hofstra University in Hempstead, New York. And it was in that class, on a frosty January morning, that I came to terms with a mysterious event in my life.

The professor began talking, in a matter-of-fact voice, about something she called "near-death experiences." Such experiences, she stressed, were so well documented that there was even a worldwide group devoted to them called the International Association for Near-Death Studies, Inc.

My thoughts whirled. Could this professor be talking about the same sort of experience I'd had years before? An experience so real, yet so bizarre, that I'd never told a soul about it? A rush of long-held-back memories flooded my mind. It seemed like yesterday.

It was spring, twenty-one years ago. I'd learned to live with a severe hearing impairment that had affected me since childhood, and I'd even earned a master's degree in special education, majoring in rehabilitation counseling. But I was very ill. The news from my doctor was devastating: acute uremic poisoning with complications. He said I had three to six months to live.

At first I didn't have the courage to reveal this prognosis to my husband, Bernie. When I told my mother, she urged that I be treated at a special clinic in Texas run by a doctor she trusted. She offered to help take care of my children, ages three and six, while I was away. So I traveled to Dr. Herbert Shelton's clinic in San Antonio, Texas. Mama and Dad took the children, and since money was tight, Bernie stayed home to work.

The clinic, in an isolated area far from the downtown and residential areas of San Antonio, was surrounded by the scrubby Texas brushland and mile upon mile of open sky. I fully expected to die there. After about three months of following a strict vegetarian diet and drinking nothing but pure water and juices, I seemed to be getting worse. I was very weak. The thought of dying frightened me, but I was so ill that I almost began to welcome death to be free from pain.

And then, on a clear September day, the most extraordinary thing happened. I left my body on the bed and was hovering up by the ceiling of my room. And then—I was outside the building. I had no more pain and was no longer aware of my body. Below me and around me was a panoramic view of the vast Texas landscape and the horizon. I seemed to be at one with the universe. I had no sense of time or space.

Next I became aware of sounds that I hadn't been able to hear without my hearing aid since I was a little girl. And what I heard was the most beautiful music— an ethereal blend of sounds, so natural as to surround me, envelop me. In addition to the music, I heard some words—the same phrase chanted over and over again. I didn't know the language, yet it was strangely familiar.

I floated and seemed to be beyond the horizon, and then in the distance appeared the graceful profile of a being with shoulder-length hair. It was a blazing silhouette from the waist up and glowing with its own most beautiful brilliant-white light. Like the music, this light seemed to surround me, envelop me, shine right through me. Although it was white, it seemed to possess all the colors of the rainbow, like the light that radiates from a perfectly cut diamond.

I was filled with a sense of wholeness and peace unlike anything I'd ever known. "The Light" I experienced was love, pure and unconditional—the "something more" that I'd yearned for since I was a child.

Now, with crystal clarity came these words: *"Baruch*

Atah Adonai . . . Baruch Atah Adonai." They were woven like a golden thread through the beautiful music that surrounded me *". . . Baruch Atah Adonai."* I had no idea what the words meant.

Then I was back in my room again, in my bed. I felt weak and racked with pain. My chest felt crushed. I couldn't breathe. And there was something terribly wrong with my left side. Dr. Shelton and some attendants crowded around my bed.

Later on I learned I had suffered an angina attack, but I would be all right. My left side was palsied, but months of intensive physical therapy enabled me to regain the use of my arm and leg; gradually my overall health improved. Three months later I was able to go home.

I wasn't brought up in a religious home. Nevertheless I sensed that I had undergone a deeply spiritual experience—something too meaningful to risk being ridiculed or diminished in any way. So I told no one, not even Bernie, about "The Light." I felt protective. The experience was too deeply personal to be shared at that time.

Then, twenty-one years later, while sitting in a college classroom with the nurturing support of about twelve of my peers, I felt a powerful sense of affirmation; I began to see a connection between the deaths that had led me to attend this class and my own near-death experience. It was an awakening.

I completed the course and plunged into advanced studies on death, dying, and bereavement. Meanwhile, I solved the puzzle of those words I'd heard. They had sounded vaguely familiar, like Hebrew, so I made an appointment with a local rabbi.

I met with him several days later in his paneled office and told him about my experience and the words. I was saying what happened for the first time—and I felt as if it had just occurred. "Rabbi," I said, "it was many years ago that I heard those words. What do they mean?"

He looked at me intently. *"Baruch Atah Adonai"* repeated the rabbi softly, stroking his chin, "means 'Blessed art Thou, O Lord.' " I gasped and repeated, *"Baruch Atah Adonai*—Blessed art Thou, O Lord." How appropriate!

Blessed art Thou, O Lord. So many nights as I drifted off to sleep, dog-tired from studying, I felt my strength and well-being restored as I recalled the magnificent "Light," the beautiful music, the reverent words.

Over the next year, I found myself increasingly drawn toward the study and practice of hospice care and counseling to help terminally ill patients and their loved ones. At the heart of hospice philosophy is understanding death as a natural part of life; an experience not to be shied away from or denied, but met with confidence and hope. The idea is to improve the quality of the life remaining to the patient and not to prolong the dying process.

Recalling Mama's, Richard's, and Aunt Julia's drawn-out battles with cancer, I understood the hospice belief that, while pain control is always necessary, in some cases a course of radical surgery or the use of heroic measures *or* extended therapy with drugs, chemicals, and radiation, may not be the best use of the time the dying patient has left.

Healing can occur on many levels, and it may not always mean a physical cure. The dying person is often in need of deep emotional and spiritual healing as well. And so is the family. "You can't learn everything about hospice work from books," explained a dear friend who is a clinical-oncology nurse specialist. "You need to be able to listen at a different level, intuitively, so you can respond to the unspoken needs of dying patients and their families and friends."

Listen at a different level. That was one thing I knew I could do after nearly half a century of living with a severe hearing loss. Many times I'd watched a person say one thing with his lips, while his eyes and face and body communicated an altogether different message.

On Christmas Day, I was nearing the end of a double shift as a volunteer in the hospice unit of one of our local hospitals. One of the patients was a middle-aged man dying of cancer; he had been hospitalized for a period of time and had become comatose.

The medical community generally agrees that, even when comatose, the patient is aware—however dimly and mysteriously—of the presence of others, aware not only of their presence, but also aware of what they are saying and doing. I explained this to the man's wife and two grown daughters as they stood in painful silence outside his room.

"He knows you're here," I said. "He knows it's Christmas Day. Come into the room. Say his name. Talk to him. Share your love for him. He will hear you." I asked his wife, her face drawn with exhaustion and grief, to stroke her husband's cheek. "Kiss his forehead," I whispered.

Death was imminent, and the man's extremities were cold and turning blue. I asked one of the daughters to take her father's hand into her own. "Hold it tightly with both of your hands," I said.

I asked the other daughter to cradle her father's feet. "Cup them in your hands and message them gently," I said. "Stroke his toes, his ankle . . . There, give him some of your warmth and life. . . ."

Then I stepped aside, over to the window. I joined the family in my mind and spirit, praying that healing would take place where it was needed, in whatever form that might be.

I saw the man's toes start to move just the tiniest bit. And then a bit more. His color began improving.

"Look!" exclaimed the daughter at his side. "He's beginning to move!"

Before leaving the room to allow the family time alone, I encouraged them to share their deepest feelings with him. "Now is your chance to complete any unfinished business you may have with one another. Now is the time to talk about love—to say words you always wanted to say but never had time to—or to ask forgiveness."

As I left, I realized that my own pain about Mama, Richard, and Aunt Julia had been eased by helping this family.

And when I returned some three-quarters of an hour later, I saw something that took my breath away. For present in that patient's room were not only the patient and his family—*but "The Light" was there too!* Filling the room with a glorious radiance, shining in our eyes, *"The Light" was with us!*

My hospice work has taught me that in this life, along with the joy, are pain, sorrow, suffering, death. But through it all, God cares. He is light—"The Light." And when God's Light breaks through our darkness, it is with a power strong enough to redeem even the most hopeless-seeming situation—even death itself. To me death is not hopeless. It is not the end.

Baruch Atah Adonai!

TWO

WHEN WE FEEL SEPARATED

*A*nd Jesus came and said to them,
"I am with you always, to the end of the age."

—Matthew 28:18, 20 NRSV

Distance and death are the great separators in our lives. Yet the apostle Paul tells us that nothing can separate us from the love of God in Jesus Christ— no measurement of any distance, and not even death (Romans 8:38–39). So it is that our feelings of grief and separation often open us up to experience God's presence and love in special and mysterious ways.

A PLACE AT THE TABLE

Peggy Eastman

*T*he fourteen-pound turkey sat ready for the oven. On the night before Thanksgiving, the plates were already stacked—eleven of them—and the knives, forks, and spoons were laid out neatly on the white lace tablecloth. I mentally ticked off the serving dishes and counted the glasses and napkins—cloth ones I'd have to wash and iron. But this was a special Thanksgiving, and paper napkins just wouldn't do.

My life was settling down after the loss of my husband in a plane crash four years earlier. The emotional scars were healing, I'd just become engaged, and I was looking forward to giving thanks for my new fiancé, Rudy. I'd even written down a short blessing to say: "Dear Lord, on this Thanksgiving day, let us bless your name without ceasing, for we know that all things good and lovely and loving come from you. Amen."

As I stood at the sink scrubbing pans, I began to feel chills. *Just tired*, I thought, continuing to work. The chills did not let up. I put on a sweater, turned up the heat. The chills got worse. My teeth were chattering and now my throat was sore. My head felt hot. All of a sudden I felt so tired I could no longer stand up. *Oh, no, not the flu. Not now. Not when I've planned everything and counted on having everyone here.*

I dragged myself up the stairs and crawled under the

quilt on my bed, fully clothed except for my shoes. But the chills wouldn't stop. Finally I picked up the phone and, with a wobbly voice, called off my special Thanksgiving dinner. "No visitors," I told my mother. "I'll just have to stay in bed and get over this." We arranged to have the turkey picked up; my sister-in-law would have the dinner. My fiancé, a widower, would have dinner with his children. A wave of sadness swept over me. My plates, glasses, and serving dishes would go unused. God would go unthanked in this silent house.

Thanksgiving day I lay in bed with my golf ball throat and my fever, alone in the house except for my dog. I reached down and stroked her thick black fur, then let her out. Tired and out of breath just from negotiating the stairs, I settled back on my pillow.

Some Thanksgiving. We were supposed to thank God for our afflictions as well as our joys, but I didn't like thanking him for the flu. I tried to remember what our prayer leader had said in church about coming closer to God when you least felt like it. She'd said, "You have to practice the presence of God. Pray as you can; don't pray as you can't."

Still angry and full of self-pity, I closed my eyes and tried to pray silently, willing my mind to center on God. But my mind rebelled. I thought about how I would have to take off the white lace tablecloth and put away the plates and serving dishes. I thought about the wash. About buying dog food. I thought about myself, and how awful the flu made me feel.

I tried again, I asked God to help me set aside my anger and self-pity. *Lord, I may be sick in bed, but I don't have the spiritual flu; please help me come closer to you.* My mind quieted. One by one I visualized the faces of those dear to me who would be celebrating Thanksgiving without me. I thanked God for them. But I yearned to be with them.

I lost all sense of time and space as my mind free-floated in prayer. My bedroom with its patchwork quilt and embroidered blue bouquet of flowers on the wall faded from my consciousness. I was not aware of breathing, of being sick. I was not aware of being.

Later, I don't know how much later, the phone rang. "It was the strangest thing," my mother was saying. My sister-in-law, she said, had miscounted and set out an extra plate. "We all felt, well, almost as if another person were here.

"And then—all of a sudden a blessing just seemed to come to me, and I said it at the table," said my mother. "I really hadn't planned it; you know how we always hold hands and say the family grace."

"Do you remember the blessing you said?" I asked quietly.

"Dear Lord," said my mother into the telephone, "let us bless your name without ceasing, for we know that all things good and lovely and loving come from you."

"Amen," I said.

"MOM, MOM!"

Carol L. Mackay

When the girls were young I could hear them calling for me at night, "Mom, Mom!" if they were sick or troubled, and I would go rushing down the hall to their bedsides. But this time when I heard the cry "Mom,

Mom!" both daughters were grown, and Kathryn was a married woman, traveling halfway around the world with her husband, Peter. Still, it was unmistakable—she was calling me.

Picking up a Bible from the nightstand, I went into the family room to pray. I had a feeling of great urgency; Kathy needed help. "Dear God, show me what to do," I prayed. Then I turned to the ninety-first Psalm, repeating it over and over again, before I was able to feel at peace.

A few weeks later we got a letter postmarked from Singapore. "I'm grateful to be able to write this," Kathy began. "I can now tell you I was quite ill in Borneo with some sort of flu. We were there, doing our usual exploring one afternoon, when I suddenly became very sick and feverish.

"Back in our room, Peter became worried. As I rambled incoherently, he searched for someone who knew of a good doctor. Finally he found a local doctor who came to our scruffy, rented room. Seeing our predicament, this good man invited us to his house, where he and his housekeeper nursed me back to health—thank God."

What touched me most came at the end of the letter. "Remember when I was a girl, and I would call out 'Mom,' and you would come rushing down the hall? That night in Borneo, in my fever, I called . . .

"And then I could hear you rushing down the hall."

ALWAYS A DREAM

Constance Foster

*M*y Uncle Bill flew an old crate in World War I, and loved every moment in the air over France. In his pocket he carried pictures of his wife and the baby son he had never seen; at night he dreamed about going home to them.

He had other dreams, too, about making this world safe for democracy. He remembered how Jane had said of him on their honeymoon, "Always a dreamer . . ." and smiled. Anyway, they were fine dreams he had of freeing people and making the world a better place for the little fellows like himself to live in. The trouble was, when he'd been back home for a while, Jane protested, he didn't do anything about making a better place for his own little fellow, Chuck, to live in.

"Just look at that backyard," she groaned, "a regular pigsty; Chuck doesn't have a decent place to play."

But my Uncle Bill and my cousin Chuck thought that the yard was a wonderful place. It was full of old wooden packing boxes they could use for make-believe airplanes to fly around the world together. Bill had placed a small one for a cockpit on top of a large one and rigged up two boards for wings.

"Look, Chuck, there's Afghanistan down there under us," Bill would point out to the four year old. Or, "We're right over Egypt now. See the Nile flowing along like a green satin ribbon?"

Sometimes Bill let Chuck take the stick alone. At four, Chuck was a rather timid little boy, clamoring earnestly, "You won't let me crack up, will you, Daddy? You'll help me out if I get in a jam?"

"Of course I won't let you crack up, son," his father assured him gravely. "You can always count on me no matter when or where."

Chuck believed it with all his heart, but nobody else figured that Bill was a man to be counted on. He held half a dozen jobs briefly and dreamed his way right out of them. Folks said he was impractical—a good man but a daydreamer. Jane had to go back to teaching school in order to support the family.

"Chuck thinks you're a hero now," she said to Bill one day. "But what will he think of you later when he finds that you can't hold even a mediocre job without fluffing it?"

That bothered Bill, for he knew it was true. Chuck was growing older now, also growing smarter. He'd soon see his dad for what he really was—only a dreamer.

So one day Bill put his toothbrush in his pocket and left town. Now and then, a postcard would come from South America or the Orient. Chuck saved every one of them; he loved the strange foreign stamps, and the adventure his father represented. He thought more of him than ever, now that he was off on a glamorous crusade of action. Then word came that Bill had joined up with the Loyalists in Spain and was flying a fighter. Chuck's heart swelled with pride. He was eighteen now, a husky six-footer.

Bill was a fool for luck—or maybe his son's prayers had something to do with it. He came through his second war without a scratch. But the old ticker was showing the combined effects of his added years and steady neglect of himself.

It wasn't until Chuck enlisted in the Air Force after Pearl Harbor that Bill came home to stay. The boy wanted it that way. Jane knew he'd been praying about a private dream of his own—having his father and mother together again. She was older now; so was Bill. The old complaints no longer mattered so much. Her teacher's pension would take care of the simple needs.

She and Bill lived for the boy's letters after he left to fly a bomber in the South Pacific. They enjoyed a new closeness that next year. Bill hadn't changed much, except to get grayer and shorter of breath. But Jane found comfort in taking care of him.

But neither of them was really living, there in the old house. They were living out on the vast expanse of the shining South Pacific. That was when they took to praying together. Maybe they were powerless, but God wasn't.

Chuck told me later about the thing that happened out there on a blazing hot day. He said he was thinking about the folks at home when he took off from the carrier on a routine bombing mission.

"It's yesterday—May 5th—back there in Centerville," he figured as he glanced at his wristwatch. "It must be about 8:00 P.M. They've finished supper and probably Dad's watering the lawn while Mom cleans up in the kitchen."

It was on the return trip that he ran into trouble. Somehow he was separated from the rest of the formation, and three enemy planes jumped on him. Their bullets killed his gunner and crippled his plane. Chuck felt his right arm go dead, and blood poured from a wound in his shoulder. Suddenly he began to black out. His head whirled. The last thing he remembered was that his father suddenly seemed to be sitting right there beside him in the cockpit. In a quiet, steady voice he was telling him just what to do.

"I won't let you crack up, son, I promised, remember? You're going to make it back to the carrier, just hold on. Ease back on your stick—a little more altitude. I have my hand on that artery. And God is here with us, too, Chuck. He's always with us wherever we are."

Chuck heard it all though a black haze. But he was doing what Bill said, holding the plane on course.

"You're a great flyer, Dad. The best."

"Just a dreamer, Chuck," the old man chuckled. "But they've been good dreams."

Somehow Chuck set the plane down on the carrier, and they lifted him out. He was unconscious from loss of blood. It was several weeks before mail from the States reached him in his hospital bed. His mother had written the letter. Chuck still has it.

"Dad had seemed so much better lately," she told him. "He'd had a heart attack, but the doctor said he was going to get over it. I went upstairs to give him his medicine at 8:00 P.M., but he was asleep. I wasn't going to rouse him, but just as I was tiptoeing out of the room he sat bolt upright in bed and said, 'Chuck needs me. I've got to go to him, Jane; I promised,' I gave him his pill and told him he'd been dreaming. 'Always a dreamer, eh?' he smiled as I tucked him in.

"When I came back an hour later he was lying there still smiling. But he was dead."

Bill had slipped away between 8:00 and 9:00 P.M. on the South Pacific, out where Chuck was in such dire need of a good flyer like his dad.

THE SIGN

William Schmitz

I was on a hunting trip that gray September afternoon when the word came that Frank was dead. Frank, our twenty-year-old son, the baby of our family. I was stunned. I wanted to scream that it couldn't be true.

But it was true. Frank had been killed instantly when the small plane he was flying had gone into a spin and crashed.

All the time during that long trip home, through my tears, I relived in my mind Frank's short life. So much had been crowded into it.

One day when he was thirteen, I found him lying in the street unconscious from multiple injuries from a motor scooter accident. He spent weeks in the hospital recovering from a skull fracture. During that time Frank had developed a deep personal relationship with God.

As Frank recovered at home, we'd catch him studying the sports pages longingly. He'd been a star baseball and football player in school, but now his damaged body seemed to rule that out. When he was finally able to limp about, he craved exercise, and I build a set of outdoor high bars for him.

After the funeral, our two older sons returned to their homes, and my wife, Polly, and I were alone in our grief. I tried to go back to work as a petroleum geologist, but it was useless. I'd sit in my office, turning a pencil over and over in my hand asking, *Why? . . . why?*

I couldn't seem to do anything anymore except think about Frank. "O God," I cried, "please give us some sign . . . some acknowledgment that he is safe with you."

But Polly and I sank deeper into our depression. One Sunday, however, we took a drive. When we returned home and I reached to turn off the ignition, Polly stiffened and clutched my arm. "Bill, look!" she gasped. She pointed to the earth below the high bars.

I could not believe what I saw. There, glowing in the late afternoon sun, stood two blood-red lilies in a place where nothing had ever grown before. They grew straight and sturdy from the earth in the same spots Frank had placed his feet to exercise.

Polly and I marveled how they got there. The area had been mowed only a day earlier. We had once placed a swing on the high bar for our grandchildren, and the trampled earth was like iron. But there they stood.

The lilies flourished for two weeks. Then they were gone.

But we didn't need them anymore to assure us that Frank was safe with God.

GOD'S FOOTPRINT

Bliss Carman
from Vestigia

I took a day to search for God,
And found Him not. But as I trod
   By rocky ledge, through woods untamed,
   Just where one scarlet lily flamed,
I saw His footprint in the sod.

"TELL MARY TO WAIT"

Beverly Fowler

*M*y father was one of eight children. His mother suffered a breakdown after the eighth child was born and was absent during their formative years. My father was five at the time, and his seven-year-old sister, Mary, became "Little Mother" to him. A closeness developed between them that lasted all their lives.

As a girl I knew there was something special about

that closeness. On certain Sundays after church, Dad would decide unexpectedly to drive to Mary's house, fifty miles away. Mother always felt Dad should let her know first, but Dad would say, "No, Mary's expecting us." Sure enough, when we arrived, the table would be set for guests and a child's chair would be ready for me. "I knew you were coming," Mary would say.

In old age, Aunt Mary retired to Florida and Dad moved to a retirement home near us in Pennsylvania. One day, though he had not spoken to her in months, Dad announced sadly, "Mary's gone." It was so. Mary had died that very morning.

One morning two years later we gathered around my father's hospital bed. We knew he had only hours to live. He looked at my mother and asked, "Is Mary still here?"

Mother was startled, and answered, "I don't know, dear."

"She was here all night." He gestured toward the head of his bed. "Tell her to wait." Those were his last words.

Of course we knew that Mary had not been there that night, but we were comforted by the thought that, close as they were, Mary would indeed be waiting for him. That would be so like her.

GLORIA'S PROMISE

Nikki McFaul

The first time I saw Gloria Marshall she was singing in the choir at Fairview Community Church, here in Costa Mesa, California. My six-year-old son, Colin, pointed her out: "Mommy, there's my Sunday school teacher." She was a small-framed woman with wispy brown hair haloing her face. And when she sang, her face purely glowed.

My husband, four children, and I were newcomers at the church, and ever since we'd joined, Colin had been raving about his teacher. I patted his hand, grateful he liked her, thankful my kids were able to have the kind of Christian experience that had been missing in my own childhood.

While my mother was a traditional Christian, my father was not. They were divorced, and I'd lived with my mother, brother, and sister in a little duplex in California. As the choir sang that Sunday morning, I recalled those days vividly, especially the year I was eight. That was when Mama got cancer. We had a picture of Jesus on our living room wall, and sometimes Mama would look at it and say that if she died Jesus would take her to heaven, where she would watch over us.

One night I awoke to find Mama bending over the double bed where all of us children were sleeping. I watched dreamlike as she kissed each of us. The next morning she was gone. She'd been taken to the hospital, where she died that same day. She was forty years old. I thought about what Mama had said, that she would go to heaven and watch over us. More than anything, I wanted assurance that it was true.

I went to live with my father. He didn't believe Mama was in heaven. He explained that her soul had gone to sleep. Period. With time and tutoring I came to believe as he did, that death was an ending, that there was no consciousness, just the mist of eternal slumber.

That's pretty much the idea I'd lived with all my life. Then a few years ago I found a deeper, personal relationship with Jesus Christ. Now I was trying to believe in God's beautiful promise of eternal life. But to be honest, it was difficult sometimes to put those deeply ingrained doubts behind me.

After the service at church that Sunday morning, I made a point to meet Colin's teacher. Gloria Marshall was a single parent with three children; she worked at a center for mentally handicapped children. As we talked, I had the compelling feeling that she was someone I should get to know better.

In the weeks to come, however, I saw her only occasionally at church functions. Then one December afternoon I plopped into a dining room chair to read the church newsletter. Inside was a note from Gloria thanking the church for supporting her as she faced a recurrence of her cancer. *Cancer?* Why, I didn't even know she was sick!

As I sat there, Tiger, our old tabby, slinked over and purred against my leg. I rubbed the cat's ear, a sudden idea nibbling in my thoughts. In my work as a stress counselor I often used positive mental imagery to help clients find healing. Maybe Gloria would consider working with me, at no charge.

She was more than willing, and we began therapy sessions in January, meeting weekly in my office and at home. Gloria and I experimented with various meditations and visualizations that would help her envision God's love and healing being released into her life. Inviting a healing image into the mind can have a powerful effect on the body, and Gloria and I kept searching for the one just right for her.

One day as we began our session, a unique, imaginative image popped into my head. "Close your eyes, Gloria," I told her. "Call up a picture of a winged horse." As she followed my direction, I said, "Imagine that he has been sent to you by God, and he can fly you anywhere you choose to go. Now climb upon his back and let him take you to your own special healing place."

Maybe it was whimsical, but after a few minutes, when Gloria opened her eyes she was more relaxed than I'd ever seen her. "Oh, Nikki," she cried. "He took me to the most beautiful garden, where I walked and talked with Christ. There were flowers and springs of water."

The winged-horse meditation became her favorite. Again and again she would travel to the imaginative garden to meet the reality of Christ's presence. During her communion she often pictured Jesus giving her "living water" from the springs along the garden paths.

As spring came and went, a bond of closeness formed between us. Best of all, Gloria improved. An exam showed her inoperable tumor was actually shrinking. "Whatever you're doing, keep doing it," her doctor said. And we did.

Meanwhile, Colin's attachment to Gloria deepened too. She became his most beloved babysitter. One weekend Gloria kept Colin so that my husband and I could get away for some time together. When we returned, Colin was quieter than usual. That night I tucked him in bed, planting a kiss on his forehead.

"Mommy, what will happen to Gloria if she dies?" he asked.

"Gloria will live in heaven with Jesus," I answered, hoping he did not sense the uncertainty in my voice.

Colin closed his eyes, but the little frown of worry remained on his face.

Gloria had been progressing for six months when the change began. Gradually I noticed her energy waning. She grew thinner. Soon the doctor confirmed my fear: The tumor was growing again.

Before long Gloria was unable to go on with our sessions. At our last one she presented me with a ceramic figure she'd made herself, a pastel blue horse. A winged horse.

"I will not give up hope, but I have to face the possibility I may die," she told me. "Perhaps the healing garden in my meditation is really heaven." She said it with such peaceful simplicity that I thought my heart would break.

"No—" I protested.

Gloria knew I struggled with doubts about the hereafter, and she interrupted me, a twinkling light in her eyes. "When I die, I'm going to be your best guardian angel, Nikki. I'll still be around; you'll see."

Autumn arrived. I threw myself into a busy schedule. I called Gloria often. Her voice seemed weak, like a sound fading in my ear. But while the leaves turned loose and drifted away, Gloria held on.

It was during the Christmas Eve service at church that I discovered her condition had suddenly worsened. After church I hurried to her house. Gloria's bed was surrounded with people speaking in hushed tones. "She's in a coma," her mother told me.

I lifted Gloria's hand into mine. "It's Nikki," I said, "I'm here. I love you." Her eyelids flickered. For a moment she seemed on the verge of speaking, then she lapsed back into her comatose sleep. I squeezed her hand and left. Outside, Christmas tree lights flickered in windows along the street. I knew I would not see Gloria again.

At home I retreated into my office, feeling desolate. Oddly, the pain of losing Gloria kept mingling with memories of my mother. I remembered that my mother had died at the same age Gloria was now, of the very same disease.

Oh, Gloria . . . I picked up the ceramic winged horse from my desk, thinking of the garden she had visited in her meditations. If only there could be a place like that!

Gloria died early Christmas morning. During the late afternoon, we attended her memorial service at the church. Gloria had requested we sing the French carol "Angels We Have Heard on High." But even when we sang the chorus, "Gloria in excelsis Deo," setting Gloria's name to angelic music, I could find little peace.

Later I stood before my bedroom window. The night was cold and starry. I gazed into the darkness for a long while, then went to bed, exhausted.

In the wee hours of the morning I awoke from a deep sleep, strangely alert. I cannot begin to explain what happened next. I simply felt what I thought to be the cat sink onto the foot of the bed against my feet. Tiger knew good and well she was not allowed on the bed. I moved my foot to nudge her to the floor, but she was not there. Then I remembered . . . I had put Tiger outside for the night.

I peered through the shadow. There was nothing on my bed at all, but the weight remained! It pressed against my feet, unmistakably, gently.

Suddenly a peculiar warmth glowed in the room as if it were enveloped by an electric blanket. My friend Gloria was there. I knew it. The certainty of it seemed indisputable to me.

I do not know how long I lay there with the mysterious pressure on the foot of my bed, but I had the overwhelming feeling that any moment I might actually see her sitting there.

Gradually, though, the weight on the bed disappeared. As it did, my mind was seized by a mental picture, like a movie playing on a screen inside my head. I saw Gloria in white, walking through a garden of unspeakable beauty, a garden blooming with bright flowers and flowing with streams of silver water. I saw her reach out her hand to a shining figure who I knew was Christ.

The image faded. I drifted into tranquil sleep.

When the alarm buzzed some hours later, the room was harsh with sunlight. I climbed from the bed, trying to come to grips with the experience of the night before. In the cold light of day, my intellect wanted a rational explanation. How could such a thing have happened? Was it some imagined illusion? Or had Gloria actually reached across the gulf to give me the assurance I needed so desperately in my life?

Bewildered, I wandered into the hallway. There I bumped into Colin, hurrying from his bedroom. His face was lit with wonder, with that special look a child gets when he sees something wonderful for the very first time.

"Mommy," he said, "why was Gloria sitting on my bed last night smiling at me?"

I gazed into his small upturned face, transfixed. Precisely at that moment I remembered Gloria's words: "When I die, I am going to be your best guardian angel. I'll still be around; you'll see."

I took Colin in my arms. "Perhaps Gloria came to assure you she is fine," I said full of certainty.

Today, two years after Gloria died, I still marvel at the glimpse of another reality that God granted to Colin and me that Christmas. I don't know why it happened. I only know I found the assurance I had longed for all my life—that death is merely a portal into another dimension, a heavenly dimension, which like the garden in Gloria's meditation, brims with beauty and life and the radiant presence of Christ.

IN MOTHER'S ARMS

Eleanor Sass

*W*hen my mother died I didn't feel depressed. Mother had lived a long and fulfilled life. Now she was with the Lord, so I felt peaceful about that. Still, I missed her a lot, and she was often in my thoughts.

Every now and then I'd dream of my father, or another deceased relative. But I never dreamed about my mother. Sometimes I wondered why. After all, I'd loved her dearly. She'd loved me. And, as far as I knew anyway, I wasn't harboring any deep-down resentments.

Years passed. Then my beloved eighteen-year-old dachshund, Heidi, died. As an unmarried woman living alone, I had no immediate family. Heidi had been my family. We'd spent a lot of time together, going for long walks, or visiting friends in the country on weekends. I'd even taken her with me on a number of my vacation trips.

The night after Heidi died I had a dream. In the dream I could see her. She was being held by someone. It was my mother.

THE LIFTED CURTAIN

Edward K. Leaton

Certain I am that God from time to time chose to reveal himself to us. Sometimes he comes to us in moments of stark drama, sometimes so softly, so unobtrusively, that only our souls seem to have seen him . . .

For many years my wife and I waged a life-and-death battle for our two sons, both of whom had muscular dystrophy. Only when the long, long struggle was over did we realize that God had revealed himself to us. Yet we would have missed his visit had it not been for a good friend, Edwin Ferree—and for our church.

Ed and Henrietta Ferree and my family belong to St. Paul's in Darien, Connecticut, and when I say "belong," I mean just that. It is part of us and we are part of it, part of the Body of Christ on earth, and, as the Bible says, "we bear one another's burdens." This is not just a pretty phrase; it is something that became a living daily reality as we watched the day-by-day, year-by-year deterioration of our two growing boys.

My son Ken was three years old when doctors diagnosed his slowness in walking as muscular dystrophy, Duchenne-type. Prognosis was for progressive deterioration of his muscles until, sometime in his teens, those muscles necessary to life itself would be affected.

A few weeks after we received this verdict, Ken's younger brother, Billy, was born, suffering from the same condition.

Several years later, Jan and I, knowing we would have Ken and Billy so short a time, determined to enjoy every day together to the utmost. And there was much to enjoy as the boys walked and talked and explored their world. But with this disease every gain is temporary. Ken, being older, was the first to move into a wheelchair. Some days I would come home to find Jan shut in an upstairs bedroom, tears streaming down her face, while downstairs the therapist painfully straightened bent legs and uncurled clenched fingers.

The strain on Jan as they grew older was enormous: toileting the two large boys, dressing them, feeding them. As Ken's circulation slowed he had to be turned in bed throughout the night. One morning I came downstairs to find Jan, head down, asleep at the dining room table; she'd been catching naps between trips to the downstairs room where the boys slept.

When Ken was fourteen, Billy, eleven, we entered them both in New Britain Memorial, a hospital specializing in long-term and terminal cases. We could probably have managed Billy at home for another year, but it seemed to us that hospitalization would be traumatic enough without separating the boys as well. Billy, with his mop of straight black hair and huge hazel eyes, had never had the muscle control of lips and tongue to speak clearly. Only Ken seemed to have no trouble understanding him. They would talk by the hour, Ken's blond head bent close to Billy's dark one, the older boy interpreting the younger one's thoughts for the rest of us. We knew they must stay together.

To Jan and me the move to the hospital was defeat, the moment we'd been dreading for so many years. But for Ken and Billy, surprisingly, it turned out to be an exhilarating change. Here, instead of being the ones who forever needed help, they discovered that they had help to give.

In the young people's wing at New Britain, everyone who possibly could attended the regular public high school in town, in wheelchairs, even on stretchers, their life-support machinery going with them via the ramps and wide doorways the townspeople had provided. Ken soon found himself helping kids all over the ward with their schoolwork.

Billy, who could still maneuver his own wheelchair, found delight in push-wheeling other young patients into the rec room or to the bedsides of friends.

Having turned our precious sons over to the care of others, and finding that their world did not collapse, Jan and I began to wonder whether in other ways we were relying too much on ourselves alone. It was at this point in our lives that we began the great experiment at St. Paul's, turning ourselves, our family, every detail of living over to the Lordship of Jesus.

It was the beginning of a whole new way of perceiving reality. Not us and our problems in a box over here, others in their separate boxes over there, but all of us at St. Paul's sharing our heartaches, our defeats and victories, together. And one of the parishioners whom we drew especially close to was Edwin Ferree. When Jan and I didn't understand some spiritual concept, when something was too hard for us, we could use Ed's understanding, Ed's strength. It was that real and simple.

Nearly four years after the boys entered New Britain, Billy caught pneumonia. The doctors saved him, but he could no longer breathe without machinery. He was moved to the Intensive Care Unit on the floor below, where his older brother could be wheeled to visit him each day.

For four months, while Ed Ferree and the others at St. Paul's supported us in prayer, Jan and I made the hundred-thirty-mile round trip to New Britain almost every evening. Our invariable routine was to visit Billy first, then go up and be with Ken.

On August 30, 1972, however, for no reason we could have explained, we went first to Ken. He was full of the visit he'd had with Billy. "They let me stay twice as long as usual because Billy's feeling so good. He wasn't even stuttering much."

Down in Intensive Care we found Billy just as Ken had said, hazel eyes shining as he watched television through the tubes and wires linking him to his life-support system. The TV was tuned to the Munich Olympics: With obvious delight he was watching the Russian gymnast, Olga Korbut. Like many disabled youngsters, Billy was fascinated by physical perfection. Olga was his heroine.

Her flawless routine ended; he turned to us. "I'm going to do all those things!" he said, pronouncing each word distinctly. "Just like she did."

It wasn't a question or a wish, it was a statement of fact.

"Billy!" cried Jan, leaning over him. "What's the matter?" His color, so ruddy a moment ago, had turned a sickly blue.

In an instant a nurse was at the bedside, then the doctor. But in spite of all they could do, Billy slipped gradually into a deep coma.

Through the long evening I kept thinking about the tenderness of God. If Ken had died first—as in the normal course of the disease he would, being three years older—stammering Billy would have been left without his link to his world. And so in spite of all medical probability the Lord was taking the younger boy first.

Peggy, the night-duty nurse came on. The clock crept to midnight . . . 1:00 A.M. . . . 2:00 A.M. And at that moment Billy's eyelids fluttered open. His hazel eyes found Jan.

"Thank you, Mom."

Then me: "Thank you, Dad."

Then they opened wider still, looking not at us, but beyond, at something we could not see. "Oh!" he cried out. Then with a joyous shout: "God!"

His eyelids closed; he was again in deep, unreachable coma. Peggy and I bent over the bed; Jan closed her eyes, praying. After about twenty minutes something like a warm breeze blew past me in the still air. The same instant Jan opened her eyes.

"Billy's gone," she said.

"I know."

At three o'clock we went upstairs and woke Ken. He made us tell over and over again about the look on Billy's face as the curtain between earth and Heaven drew aside. When the day nurse came on Ken asked her, "Can I be the one to tell the kids about Billy? I want to tell them he wasn't afraid and I'm not going to be either."

Before leaving the hospital we telephoned Ed Ferree

who had given us so much support. How glorious to tell him that we knew Billy was with Jesus.

I kept wondering if Billy were already swinging from the high bars in some heavenly arena. Backflips, somersaults, handstands . . . just like Olga.

And then a year and a half later, we were driving home from New Britain one final time. Nineteen months had passed since Billy's death. Time for Ken to graduate from New Britain High, to cast his vote by absentee ballot, to handle his lonesomeness by befriending new youngsters entering Memorial, especially those with speech defects: "I can understand him, nurse. You see, he talks a lot like my little brother did."

That afternoon, March 23, 1974, Ken had died. Only—this time—Jan and I had not been there. We had arrived at the hospital around 3:30 on a perfectly routine visit, to be told that Ken had passed away very unexpectedly an hour before.

Why? I wondered, all the long drive home. Why couldn't we have got there one little hour sooner? I turned off the parkway at our home exit. I'd been so sure that the Lord would give us some new reassurance, some fresh glimpse of his Presence, when Ken had to leave us, too.

I pulled into our driveway. What were we going to tell the people at church, this time? I'd phone Ed Ferree; he'd help us think of what to say. Inside the house I dialed the number as slowly as I could. This would be as big a shock to Ed as to us.

"Ed Ferree speaking." There was his voice on the line.

"We're just back from New Brit . . ."

"Ken's with Jesus," said Ed.

It was a moment before I could find my voice. "Yes, Ed. But how could you . . . ?"

"It happened at 2:30," said Ed. He hadn't been thinking about Ken especially, in fact he was down in his study digging some papers out of a drawer, when all of a sudden it was as though a movie were unrolling on a screen in front of his eyes. There before him was Ken, tall and straight, striding like a long-distance hiker up a grassy hillside, his blond hair glowing like gold in the bright air.

Then, as Ed watched, Ken came to a swift-flowing stream and stopped, apparently uncertain how to get across. At that moment Ed saw coming down the hill a shining figure that he knew to be Jesus. The radiant Being came to the edge of the stream and stretched his hand across to Ken. Ken reached out, clasped it, stepped easily across. The next moment both had turned and were climbing the hill together, hand in hand.

"That's what you called to tell me, wasn't it?" said Ed. "Ken is with Jesus."

The unfinished feeling disappeared. God had lifted the curtain once again. For a moment I had simply forgotten that Jan and I no longer had to depend on our own sight alone, that we had many eyes and hearts with which to know him.

"Yes, Ed," I said. "That's what I called to say."

GOD FASHIONED A HOUSE

Author Unknown

Weep if we may—bend low as ye pray!
What does it mean?

Listen! God fashioned a house. He said:
   "Build it with care."
Then softly laid the soul . . .
   To dwell in there.

And always he watched it—guarded it so,
   Both day and night:
The wee soul grew as your lilies do,
   Splendid and white.

It grew, I say, as your lilies grow,
   Tender and tall;
Till God smiled, "Now the house is too low
   For the child, and small."

And gently he shut the shutters one night,
   And closed the door;
"More room and more light to walk upright
   On a Father's floor."

THREE

WHEN WE BELIEVE

*J*esus said to him, "All things can be done for the one who believes."

—Mark 9:23 NRSV

God promises to act in response to our faith. When we commit our lives to him, believe that he will work and act accordingly, God will do what seems impossible. Sometimes we have to be jolted in order to exercise that faith, as several people whose stories appear here discovered. But when we believe and obey, we can prove the truth of what Alice Lindsay discovered: "I did not make a mistake in obeying God when he asked me to believe him, trust him and prove him."

"PROVE ME NOW"

Alice A. Lindsay

*B*ring ye all the tithes into the storehouse, that there may be meat in mine house, and prove me now herewith, said the Lord of hosts."

Prove God? Put him to the test? At first the idea seemed utterly presumptuous that a young Oklahoma housewife and mother like me should dare to dare God to prove himself. Yet that is what Malachi 3:10 was suggesting, and that very verse became the springboard to one of the most profound spiritual experiences of my life.

The year was 1934, one of the terrible Depression years. My husband, Corwin, was fortunate: He had a job. Corwin was an automotive electrician, a mechanic, and he received nine dollars for a week's work; a week being seventy-two hours in six days. We had two children, Betty Ellen and David, and though we felt ourselves fortunate to have food on the table, there was no money, none whatsoever, left over for extras.

Our living conditions were meager, even by 1934 standards. In our little three-room house we used kerosene for cooking and lights, coal for heat, and borrowed a neighbor's telephone in emergencies. Our one luxury was running water and bathroom facilities.

Our lives revolved completely around our church, not because we had acquired a deeper love for the Lord—

that love was always there—but because there was no money for amusements or other social outlets. It bothered me, however, that I could not do more for the church.

From the time that I had accepted Christ as my personal Saviour until the Depression hit us hard, I had believed in—and practiced—tithing. This had not been difficult when there was money for the necessities of life with a little left over. But now, when pennies were counted as dollars, we had to stop. I felt that God would understand.

Then something happened. One evening as I was studying my Sunday school lesson I found my entire mind and spirit suddenly come alive as I read that passage in Malachi about tithing that said "and prove me now herewith, saith the Lord of hosts."

God knows that I love him, I thought. *He knows I am doing all I can to serve him. He knows that nine dollars a week, thirty-six dollars a month, for a family of four is not a living, just a bare existence.* Prove God by reducing that amount by three dollars and sixty cents a month? Would God require that from the small, inadequate amount that I had for my family?

I just couldn't understand why I was so torn apart by that verse of scripture. I spent a long night searching my soul and praying. How unrealistic it seemed for God to ask me to surrender a part of the very little I had when he could provide so very much for us—indeed he had told us of the abundance he intended for us: "Give and it shall be given unto you; good measure, pressed down, shaken together and running over . . ." (Luke 6:38).

The first thing he did say was "give." Even the widow with her mite had done that—she had given everything—yet I was asked to give but a tenth. In my mind I saw him taking a small amount and multiplying it, the way he took a few loaves and fed thousands of people. I wondered what he might do with my tithe.

By morning, when that long night was over, I knew that he was not asking me to *test* him; what he was asking me to do was *trust* him.

On Saturday, as I did each week, I took my husband's salary of nine dollars and carefully allocated it for the following week's needs. With new determination I put first on my list: tithe, ninety cents. When I came to the end of my absolute needs I was twenty cents short of having enough for the children's milk. Milk was five cents a quart, and they must have a quart a day to be properly fed. I went over my list again. Each item had been cut to the minimum. There was only one thing I could do—reduce the tithe by twenty cents. Surely God would understand. I started to change the nine to a seven, but in that instant I felt as though someone had slapped my hand. I could not do it. The words "Prove me! Prove me!" kept burning through my mind. I closed my eyes and said, "All right, God. I will."

The following morning when I dropped God's ninety cents into the offering plate, a wonderful peace came over me. I knew that somehow God was going to take care of everything.

On the following Tuesday morning my last five cents had been spent for milk. My children faced four days without, and yet I found myself going about my work with a joyful anticipation that I could neither describe nor understand.

About eleven o'clock there was a knock on my front door. Answering it, I was confronted by a pleasant, smiling man who introduced himself as Ralph Gibson. He said he had worked with my husband about six years before and had come by to pay back a long overdue loan that he owned Corwin. With that he pressed a bill into my hand and started to leave.

It was a five-dollar bill, and I was so stunned I'm not sure I even said, "Thank you." The only thing I remember clearly was standing on my porch, holding a five-dollar bill in my hand, watching a stranger walk out of my yard as I said, "Thank you, God!"

An hour later when my husband came home for lunch, he kissed me and asked the reason for my radiant face.

When I told him, he said: "Honey, there just has to be some mistake. I just barely remember Ralph Gibson, and I'm sure I never lent him money. There just has to be some mistake."

"Ralph Gibson may have made a mistake in thinking he owed you five dollars," I said. "You may be making a mistake in having lent it to him and forgotten it. But the fact that this is a genuine five-dollar bill and I have it in my possession is not a mistake. Neither is it a mistake that the children will have not only milk for the rest of the week, but some badly needed clothing as well. And the most wonderful truth of all is that I did not make a mistake in obeying God when he asked me to believe him, trust him, and prove him."

Many times and in many ways since then God has taught me many things through his Word, and through the personal touch of his Holy Spirit. But this one lesson will always be, for me, one of the great forward steps in faith. Faith in not only God's goodness, but in his loving, caring providence for all who will dare to trust him.

MIRACLE ON THE HOMOSASSA

Nelson Hutchinson

*B*ack in those days, our family was very poor. We lived in a small house on the Homosassa River, four miles upstream from the Gulf of Mexico. My father struggled to make ends meet as a commercial fisherman.

To help, my mother and I would gather oysters when they were in season. Other times, we went into the woods and chopped fallen trees into firewood, which we sold to the people in town. On good days, we could make a dollar or two.

This was 1939. It was a bad time. A lot of people were poor. The fortunate people who had jobs earned thirty cents an hour.

That year, my mother joined a church in town. There was no road from our house into town. To get there, we had to go by boat three more miles upstream to the highway and the little village. Even so, my mother was at the church every time the doors opened. She loved the church. It gave her a certain strength that carried her through the ordeal of raising a family in such dark days.

We didn't have a Bible in our home. We couldn't afford one. This was a great sadness for my mother. Week after week, she tried to put a few coins aside, saving for enough to buy a Bible, but time and again some emergency would come up, and she had to use the money for food or clothes or medicine. She never complained, but her face showed her hunger for the Word of God in our house.

One day my father came home from work with an empty boat. He had caught nothing. He went into the house discouraged, as though he never wanted to look at the river again.

I watched my mother. She got into the boat, arranged the nets, started the motor, and headed downstream. As she later told me many times, she went about a mile toward those vast, shallow flats that reach as far as the eye can see at the mouth of the Homosassa. She cut off the motor. Then she knelt in the bow of the little boat, and she began talking to God.

"Father," she said, "I want a Bible for my home and my children. We don't have any money, and so I need your help. Let me catch some fish today and I'll take them to the market and buy a Bible before nightfall. I have been working hard, trying to get enough ahead to buy a Bible, but I can't seem to make it. Anything I catch today will be yours. Please help me."

She started the motor. Standing up, she threw into the water the staff that held one end of the net. Slowly she moved the boat in a circle to close off the net. Even before she had gone halfway, fat mullet began jumping into the net. And by the time she had completed the circle, the trapped area was alive with flouncing fish. My mother had lived on the river over a dozen years, ever since she had married my father at the age of sixteen, and she had never seen anything like this.

As fast as my mother could empty her catch into the boat, the net filled up again. In an hour, there was hardly enough room in the boat for herself and the net. She headed home.

I was on the dock as my mother arrived. The boat

was riding so low in the water that I wondered if it had sprung a leak. Then I saw the cargo. I couldn't believe my eyes.

"Come on," Mother called to me. "We're going into town to get our Bible."

We went upstream to the highway, where we borrowed a cart from a farmer, transferred the catch into it, then hurried into town to a wholesaler who sold fish to stores and restaurants. The scales showed that my mother had brought in nearly three hundred pounds of fish. The wholesaler paid three cents a pound for the catch—almost ten dollars, as well as my father could do during a good, seven-day week.

We went directly to a bookstore and bought the best Bible the money could buy. My mother let me carry the Bible as we went back to the river and returned the cart. She let me hold it on my lap as she maneuvered the boat back to our home. That evening, my mother read aloud to us from her own Bible for the very first time.

After nearly forty years, the Bible is still in our family, a bit tattered now from so much use. Every morning, my mother would read the Bible to herself; every evening, she would read aloud to the family. We children studied the Bible as we prepared for our Sunday school classes. And my mother never tired of telling people how she had acquired it.

In December 1976, my parents celebrated their golden wedding anniversary. In the special ceremony at our church, my mother and my father held the family Bible between them—living proof that the miracles of the Bible can come alive today for those who have faith enough to believe in them.

GOD'S DEMANDS

Author Unknown

He never asks me to go anywhere He has not gone,
To face anything He had not faced,
To love anyone He does not love,
Or to give anything He has not given.

HIS TWO STRIPS OF WHEAT

Betty Munson

*W*e had never tithed until that year, that disastrous year.

Before then, if my husband, Cliff, or I had any loose change in our pockets, well, that was our children's Sunday school offering. We might have given a dollar when the offering plate was passed around. We are farmers, dependent on the unpredictable weather and a lot of other things that can ruin you before you know it. We had to watch out for ourselves first. God got what was left over.

Then one Sunday our pastor began talking about

tithing. Not your usual stewardship homily, but a series of sermons—almost like talks, neighbor to neighbor—based on the scriptural injunction to give back to the Lord. Something stirred within Cliff and me during those sermons, as if seeds planted long ago were finally sprouting.

I remembered a novel I'd read when I was in my teens. It was about a man who gave lovingly to his fellowman and encouraged others to do so by his example. I'd been impressed. Not because God gave to him so abundantly in return. No, I was impressed because the point of the story was to show how selfless giving, in and of itself, is pleasing to God.

Not long before we were married, Cliff had read a stirring book about the remarkable industrialist R. G. LeTourneau, a man of faith and great success in business. Cliff was struck by how LeTourneau's commitment to God was so complete that not even his work was separate from his faith. LeTourneau considered God his business partner and was a generous tither.

But we still had plenty of questions about tithing. Because we were dry-land wheat farmers, half our ground was fallowed every summer to conserve the soil moisture in this northern Montana climate. Our income was determined by how well the crop did on the other half of our acreage, and on fluctuating market prices. And of course the strength of the crop itself depended in most part on the weather. Ten percent sounded like an awful lot, especially when we considered how rarely there was anything left over after we got done with all the bills. We just didn't see how we could swing it. Yet it seemed that God always provided for us no matter what we gave in return. We knew we could do more.

We called our pastor over to the house. He explained that we could start small, not the full ten percent. The pledge card, he told us, was not a hard and fast legal agreement with the church but rather a promise to God that we would share with him the fruits of our labor. The bond was between God and ourselves.

Rather than wait until the crop went to market at fall harvest and then figure up our tithe that way, we decided we'd simpy set aside part of our acreage. We called it crop-tithing.

"I reckon two strips ought to be about right," Cliff calculated one day near the beginning of the year. A strip of wheat on our place is a half mile to a mile long—running north to south to protect the topsoil from the prevailing west winds—and maybe eighteen rods wide, a rod being roughly sixteen feet. In a good year we get a yield of twenty bushels or so per acre. We chose a couple of strips on the east end of our producing land. Come fall the yield from these strips would be our tithe. "These two are yours, Lord," I said.

After we signed our pledge card, Cliff and I felt real good about it. In fact, we began tithing some right away from the little outside work Cliff picked up before harvest season.

But then disaster struck, the kind of thing farmers have nightmares over. An early summer hailstorm cut and pounded our fledgling wheat crop into the ground. Wiped it out. The damage was total. We lost everything. Everything, that is, except those two strips on the east end, the ones we'd crop-tithed. They were unscathed.

Surveying the devastation, I felt the hurt lodge in my throat. I couldn't even cry. I was numb. What would we do now? We had no crop insurance. There would be no income for our family this year. None, unless we used those two remaining strips—two out of thirty!—for ourselves.

"Well," sighed Cliff as we disconsolately kicked

through the broken stalks and brown puddles, "we promised those to God."

I nodded. "That still has to be our tithe," I agreed. "There's no going back on it that I can see."

Cliff hooked his arm around my waist. "We'll make do," he said, squinting across our ravaged land. But neither of us could say how.

From that July until next harvest was the toughest financial time we ever had. It wore us down sometimes. But we started to learn to trust in God for every need, every problem. And there were problems.

Cliff went to the bank to borrow operating expenses till the next crop. New management had taken over. Our records had been misplaced. There was no personal relationship to fall back on. Other farmers had to borrow too. The bank lent us the money eventually, but not as much as we thought we needed.

When harvest came that autumn it was a dark period. We cut the two strips, sent the wheat to market and gave the proceeds as our tithe, just as we'd pledged. It made no sense financially, but we couldn't break our bond.

We managed. Cliff went custom cutting that fall, which means hiring out your services to other farms. He had to go farther away than usual, where there were still crops. That winter he worked repairing engines and machinery. Cliff had always been a good mechanic and we'd set him up a nice workshop. The jobs always seemed to come when things looked particularly bleak.

When farmers get in trouble in an area, a lot of other businesses suffer. But our local grocer was still able to help out by letting us charge when we had to. I only bought bare necessities on credit. Christmas that year was looking bleaker and bleaker until Cliff finished a repair job ahead of schedule. We were able to purchase a few inexpensive gifts for the kids.

Naturally I yearned for our usual ample turkey to preside at the center of the holiday table with all the trimmings. This year I couldn't bring myself to charge one. It was not a strict necessity. I didn't even pray for a turkey. I just *yearned*.

Then, on Christmas Eve, a friend showed up at our door with a big turkey as a bonus payment for some work Cliff had done. The turkey was the best-tasting bird we ever had. It was one of our best holidays too, because we felt truly blessed, maybe even more blessed than if we'd had a bumper crop to celebrate.

The Lord was taking care of us.

That winter the soles of our five year old's shoes gave out. We prayed. Soon enough Cliff got an extra job that brought in just enough for new shoes. It seemed always to happen that way during the year after our crop was wiped out. We didn't have close to what we were used to, but with prayer and with trust we always managed, and we learned to get by on what was provided.

The greatest blessing of all that year was not material. It was spiritual. God protected us from fear, from worry; for the more we trusted in him, the more our faith grew that he would watch over us always. Those two tall strips of sturdy wheat that we crop-tithed, *they* sealed that trust.

Malachi the prophet proclaimed, " 'Bring the full tithe into the storehouse, so that there may be food in my house, and thus put me to the test, says the LORD of hosts; see if I will not open the windows of heaven for you and pour down for you an overflowing blessing (3:10 NRSV).

Ever since that harvest we have tithed a portion of our crops. In good seasons and bad, it is a promise that we keep. It is a promise God returns abundantly, always.

DOUBT

William Blake

(*from* Auguries of Innocence)

He who doubts from what he sees
Will ne'er believe, do what you please.
If the sun and moon should doubt,
They'd immediately go out.

ADRIFT

Sandy Feathers-Barker

Nothing, it seemed, could spoil that hot, windy day in June. At 10:00 A.M. my husband, Joe, and I pulled out of the driveway of our apartment in Gainesville, Florida, where Joe was getting his master's degree in architecture. Trailing behind our camper-truck was our sixteen-and-a-half-foot sailboat. We were headed for Cedar Key on Florida's Gulf Coast.

"Just think, a whole afternoon of sailing," I said. Gringo, our big cinnamon-brown dog, wagged his tail. Joe whistled. The day was starting so perfectly.

If anything at all threatened to mar the day it was the

problem we'd wrestled with for weeks. Joe would finish graduate school in a couple of months, and after that, life curled up into big question marks: Where should we settle? Which job should we take? I'd worried till I was in knots. But now, as we bounced along the highway, I shoved aside my anxieties about the future. They could wait till I returned.

We arrived at the marina with the sun burning at high noon. As I stepped from the truck, a strong gust of wind squalled through the parking lot. I gazed out at the choppy blue water. A few emerald islands dotted the bay. And beyond that, the Gulf stretched to the horizon, immense and awesome. A peculiar feeling swept through me. Not really foreboding, just uneasiness.

We threw a twelve-ounce bottle of water in the boat, strapped on bright orange life jackets, and slid our sailboat into the water. "Hop on, Gringo," I called. Within minutes the three of us were careening out into the bay. I leaned over the side of our little turquoise boat to steady it against a fresh wind howling from the northeast.

Suddenly we slammed aground on a sandbar. I listened as the sand grated against the boat, hoping the centerboard wouldn't be damaged. Without that slim three-foot stabilizer that serves as a keel, we would lose practically all control.

"I'll shove us off," Joe yelled, pushing with an oar. Suddenly we broke free. Joe struggled to tack to the deeper channel waters. But something was wrong. The boat side-slipped through the blue-green swells like a car without a driver. The centerboard was obviously damaged. I wondered how badly. We were sliding sideways out of the bay! There was only one last island between us and open sea. The shoreline was shrinking to a green strip in the distance.

"Joe! We're passing the last island!"

"Don't worry, we'll make it," he said. Joe . . . always the optimist.

But around the island, the wind was even wilder. With windswept water slashing over our boat's sides, we were being pitched from wave to wave. I grabbed for terrified Gringo. "Lord," I whispered, "I think we're going to need your help." But the gale seemed to tear the words away from my mouth.

Joe seized the anchor and threw it over. "Oh, no!" I screamed as the anchor line tore from its cleat. The rope snaked overboard and disappeared forever.

"Got to get the sails down," Joe shouted over the wind, "or we'll be blown out to sea!" In our haste we did lower them, but we knocked a fitting loose and lost the halyard that we'd need to raise the sail later.

We looked at each other in horrified silence. The only way we could hoist the sail again would be to lower the hinged mast to the deck and re-rig the line from its top. And that required a calm sea and no wind at all.

In desperation, Joe fitted oars into the oarlocks and tried to row. It was hopeless. We reeled on like a toothpick in a torrent. Now the sun was sinking into a fading orange haze. Night was coming . . . darkness on the ocean. I looked back toward land. It was gone. We were lost, blown into the open sea.

Soon darkness surrounded us. Black waves crashed against the boat, showering us with cold water. I shivered in the night wind. Joe helped me wrap up in the sails and we huddled in the cramped, decked-over cockpit area beneath the mast. The boat pitched so violently that we had to lash ourselves down with ropes to keep from going overboard. My body pounded the hard hull of the boat till I ached.

Then seasickness struck. All night as we slid through the dark, twisted labyrinth of water, I lay in agonizing nausea. I wondered . . . was anyone, anywhere, looking for us?

As dawn filtered into a Sunday sky and the relentless wind still blew, I looked out at the most terrifying sight of my life. Water. Everywhere. Like a jagged gray blanket, it stretched on forever.

"Joe, where are we?" I asked.

"We're a long way out," he said grimly. "We were blown southwest."

The sun became a white-hot laser. I licked my parched lips. "We'll have to save our water," Joe said, as he measured out a few sips. I drank, watching Gringo lick the salt water on the boat. How long could we last on twelve ounces of water in this heat?

Hours went by. I craned my neck, searching for an airplane. Not even a seagull flew this far out. Our boat became a tiny floating island of hopelessness. I remembered the anxieties of yesterday. What to do after Joe finished graduate school suddenly seemed such a small, petty uncertainty.

The waves rolled by like the years of my life. Unconsciously, I laid my hand on Gringo's head. He turned his huge brown eyes up to mine. As I stared down into Gringo's eyes, something profound, yet simple, took place. I saw the look of trust, trust that, despite everything, I was taking care of him, as always. And like an arrow, a thought came to my mind. *Why shouldn't I trust God just as Gringo was trusting me?*

Across the boat Joe was saying, "We're helpless. If only we could raise the sails again, but it's impossible with the wind and waves this rough."

The thought returned: *Trust.*

I spoke slowly, hesitantly. "Do you remember in the Bible when the disciples were caught in a storm on the Sea of Galilee?"

Joe looked at me strangely. "Go on."

"Jesus calmed the wind and waves for them," I said. "If he did it for the disciples, wouldn't he do it for us?"

So while the sun glowed low and golden on the ocean, we joined hands and prayed. "Please, Lord, we're trusting you to still the wind and water. Amen." Three minutes passed. Four. Five. And then, in a moment so awesome I can still scarcely believe it, the six-foot swells melted into a sheet of still water. The wind stopped abruptly. There wasn't a ripple or a sound.

Frantically we lowered the hinged mast to the deck and retrieved the line for hoisting the mainsail. "It'll work now," Joe said, raising the mast.

Our sails slatted in the still air. "Lord," I said "we're ready. Please give us wind to blow us back east to shore."

As if the Creator's hand were moving across the sea, a steady wind began to blow. The sun hovered on the water. We were sailing away from it, east toward land! "Praise God," I rasped.

The moon rose in front of us. Since the wind was from the west, we could run before it with no need for our useless centerboard. For twelve hours, Joe clutched the rudder and the line controlling the mainsail. We guessed we'd been blown over a hundred miles out to sea. Yet, if this wind held, we could make land again.

As daylight approached, Joe neared complete exhaustion. We both collapsed in the tiny cockpit to sleep. When we awoke, the sea was a mirror of glass, the world an eerie vacuum of silence. The sails hung limp. What had happened to our east wind?

"What does it mean?" I asked. Joe shook his head. Gringo paced nervously. Fear mounted in me like a tidal wave. Was this the calm before the storm I'd always heard about?

Trust me, came the silent assurance. Trust? Stranded, without land in sight, our water gone, our bodies near collapse, and maybe a storm coming. Suddenly, it seemed too much to ask.

Joe crawled into the cockpit in despair. Even he, the eternal optimist, knew. We had reached the end.

I stared at the sea, too desolate to cry. "God," I whispered, "I was counting on you . . ." I stopped, my breath suspended. For in the distance, coming over the horizon was a cross. I rubbed my eyes and looked again. It was still there. A breathtaking white cross! It seemed to be rising straight out of the water. Was I hallucinating? Seconds later a boat rose beneath the cross. It was a cross-shaped mast. Dear God! It was real! My breath came back in muffled little gasps. A dazzling white boat was plowing right at us.

"Joe," I called, hardly able to find my voice. "A boat!" Joe leaped up, his eyes incredulous. As it churned closer, Joe raised his life jacket to the top of the mast, I waved my arms wildly.

Soon, a fifty-one-foot yacht was before us. Up on deck, an astonished boy peered down at us. "What in the world are you doing way out here?" he called.

I burst into tears as a vacationing doctor and his family appeared on deck and helped us aboard. We gathered around their table below, while the doctor checked his charts. He returned, shaking his head. "The course I set this morning on automatic pilot was eighteen miles off. An eighteen-mile deviation, I can't explain it."

But I could. There in the safe, solid cabin of the doctor's boat, it all ran together. The calming of the ocean, the sudden east wind, then its abrupt ceasing, an eighteen-mile alteration on sophisticated electronic navigation equipment—all this had made their big yacht and our little sailboat intersect exactly in the midst of endless time and water. God—a powerful, ingenious, caring God—had been there through every uncertainty . . . including those small, worrisome anxieties about the future still waiting for us at home.

A few hours later a storm smashed into the Gulf, twisting the sea into savage ten-foot waves. But I leaned back, enveloped in the thundering sound of the storm, at peace. My future, like the sea, rested in very good hands.

NOT ONE, BUT TWO

Samuel Hooker

*B*ack when I was pastoring a church in Portland, Oregon, I received a call early one morning from the local hospital. A patient who was dying had asked for a minister of my denomination. Could I come to the hospital as soon as possible?

Half an hour later I was standing at the bedside of Felix Richy as the nurse drew the curtain around us.

"Pastor," Mr. Richy said, "my uncle was a preacher, and he used to talk to me about the Lord; but I wouldn't listen. My wife always tried to get me to go to church, but I wouldn't go. Now I'm going to meet my Maker, and my life is filled with sin."

"Mr. Richy," I began, "the fact that you admit you've

sinned and are willing to confess it is half the battle."
We talked. I quoted some scripture about God's forgiveness, and then we prayed together as he turned his life
over to the Lord.

The next day I returned, and the next day, and the
next; and to the amazement of the hospital staff, Felix
kept improving. In a matter of weeks he was sent home,
and on the next Sunday he appeared in my church. For
eight years he sat in the same pew each Sunday with
hardly a miss. In the end he died suddenly of a heart
attack.

I officiated at the funeral, and after the burial an
elderly man approached me.

"Pastor Hooker," he said, "you don't know me, but I
was in the bed next to Felix Richy when you came to
the hospital that morning. I wrote down those scriptures
you quoted and gave my heart to Jesus too.

"That morning you didn't catch just one fish, you
caught two. I jumped into the net while you were
pulling it in."

FOUR

WHEN WE PRAY

*A*sk, and it will be given you. . . . For everyone who asks receives."

—Matthew 7:7, 8 RSV

Faith and prayer are inextricably mixed. We express our faith in our prayers as well as in our actions. There are times, though, when we pray with only the tiniest bit of faith. Even then, promised Jesus, "impossible" results will come. Because we pray, God meets our needs—for things as big as a baby mattress and as small as a wheel bolt. His answers show us that, as Isaiah put it, "The arm of the Lord is not too short to save, nor his ear too dull to hear" (59:1 NIV).

THAT OLD PICKUP TRUCK

Don Bell

One winter years ago, I wouldn't have said I knew much about praying, but I guess I knew where to turn when I needed help. At the time, Joe Spurgin and I were batching on the Nielson Ranch south of Cody, Wyoming. He was a ranch hand and I was a cowboy, and we were left in charge of feeding and caring for the livestock while the ranch manager, Bill Hill, was away.

When I woke up one February morning it must have been twenty below zero. I knew I had to chop ice for the cows' drinking water. I spent most of the day doctoring the animals that were sickly. Then, while Joe stayed back at the bunkhouse, I rode my horse into an area called Oregon Basin to check on the cattle there. Toward evening I headed home, eager for the hot supper Joe would have ready to eat.

I wasn't far from the ranch when I knew something was wrong. No smoke was coming out of the chimney, no sign of Joe. I put up my horse in the barn. Walking away from the stall, I saw blood frozen on the ground. I thought Joe must have butchered a beef. Then in the tack room I saw Joe Spurgin himself, lying on his back with a rifle next to his right arm. I knelt down to check his pulse. It was real weak, but Joe was still alive. *I've got to get him to the hospital,* I thought, *and quick!*

On the ranch we had an old Chevrolet pickup truck. Trouble was, it was hard to start. In the middle of summer we had to push and pull it to get it running, but in the below-zero winter, I could never tell what it would do. I rushed outside, panting in the cold air, and as I ran I said to God, "Please help me start it so I can save Joe Spurgin."

I slid onto the cold leather seat, slammed the door, blew on my hands for warmth, put my foot on the gas pedal, and turned the key in the ignition. I couldn't believe my ears. No sputter, no cough! The engine started with one turn of the key.

"Thank you, God," I whispered. "Just keep the engine running." I jumped out, lowered the tailgate and ran back to get my wounded partner.

Now, Joe was a big man, six feet tall and over two hundred pounds. With his long johns, wool shirt, jeans, cowboy boots, overshoes, coveralls, and a heavy sheepskin coat, add another twenty-five. How was a man of my size, five feet seven and one hundred forty pounds, going to move this body? "Lord," I prayed, "you helped me get that old pickup started. Now I have another favor to ask. Help me move my friend."

Before I tried to lift Joe's body, I saw he was frozen down in his own blood. I picked up a shovel, slipped it under where the blood had frozen his clothing to the barn's wooden floor and pried him loose. Joe was still unconscious. "Don't die on me," I said, and then somehow I managed to hoist him on my shoulders.

I slipped him into the back of the truck, shut the tailgate, and drove wild and fast to the Cody hospital. It was dark by the time I got there.

I backed up to the emergency room door, ran into the hospital, and was met by a doctor I knew well, Dewitt Dominick. I told him in an excited tone of voice that I had a man in my truck who was shot with a .25 caliber Winchester rifle.

Two helpers took a gurney out to the truck and loaded what I feared was a dead man onto it. Then the doctor looked him over and said, "Yep, he's alive. Just barely."

Joe's clothing was cut off him and the doctor found that Joe has been shot in the back of his right knee. The bullet came out of his ankle. Joe was still pale and unconscious, but I had to leave him at the hospital and get back to look after the ranch.

I put in a sleepless night. Next morning I got up early, fed the cattle, and took care of the ranch chores. I cleaned up, shaved, grabbed a cup of strong black coffee, and went outside to the pickup. Once again I slid onto the leather seat, slammed the door, put my foot down on the accelerator, and turned the key in the ignition.

Nothing. I sat there for a minute, then smiled. *Lord, I thought, you helped me when I needed it most. I can get to the hospital just fine without this old pickup. You just keep old Joe alive.*

I went out to the road to hitchhike and in a few minutes caught a ride that took me straight to the hospital. Joe was sitting up in bed, smiling. He'd had several pints of blood pumped into him and now a shade of color was back in his face.

"How'd it happen?" I asked.

"Don, after you rode off yesterday I saw a coyote near the sheep pen. I ran to the barn and grabbed the rifle that hangs in the tack room. And that's all I remember. I must have fainted dead away when I saw all that blood." He shook my hand and thanked me for saving his life.

Joe got well, but after that he never came back to the ranch to work. I lost track of him for a while, then heard that he went to Cañon City, Colorado, where he was employed at the state prison. He retired after twenty years and moved back to Billings, Montana, where he had a sister nearby. Then one day the sister called me and asked if I could come see Joe. He was dying and had asked for me.

I drove up to Billings and found Joe looking as gray as he did when I discovered him on the barn floor. Again Joe shook my hand and thanked me for saving his life. He gave me his hat, his silver belt-buckle, and all the money he had left in the world, $150.

"No," I said, "I don't want your money, Joe."

"Take it, partner," he said. "I'm going to die tonight. I'm going to see God, and when I get there I'm going to thank him for giving me thirty more years to live."

Joe died that night, and all these years I've kept his hat and buckle. They remind me of an old friend and an old Chevy pickup truck, and they remind me that God gives you help just when you need it most.

"Don't Let It Rain Today"

Kennith Bishop

At last, after holding Sunday school in the choir loft and in corners of the sanctuary, the members of our small church finally raised enough money to build an education building.

On the day the concrete floor was to be poured, I woke up at 5:00 A.M. Seeing the sky heavy with clouds, I phoned the contractor to call off the day's work. Rain mixing with the fresh concrete might add an additional expense that our tight budget would not permit. Our dream of a new building might be delayed indefinitely.

By 6:00 A.M., however, with no rain, I made the difficult decision to call and tell the contractor to come after all. But when I arrived at the church to await the workers, rain clouds swirled overhead. I walked to the center of the building site and knelt.

"Don't let it rain today, Lord," I prayed.

Then, thinking about the farmers in this rural community who needed the rain, I changed my request. "Just don't let it rain right here."

Within a few minutes, the crews arrived and prepared the ground for the concrete. The clouds grew more ominous. At noon the workers drove away for lunch. Soon they returned to report that the rains were coming down so hard around them, they couldn't get out of their trucks.

In the afternoon the men worked feverishly, hurrying to finish before the expected downpour. To the east and to the west, rain pounded down.

But that day, on the site where the concrete was poured, the rains never fell.

OUR REFUGE

Nina Willis Walter

Whenever you come to the Lord
   with an earnest prayer,
He is there.

When you come with a contrite heart
   or a human fear,
He will hear.

Though you may have little to give,
   bring Him your best;
He supplies the rest.

THE MIRACLE MATTRESS

John Cowart

We kept our newest baby in an egg carton—not one of those Styrofoam ones with pockets for a dozen eggs, naturally, but the large cardboard box that hundreds of eggs come in. My resourceful wife had covered the box with some flannel material printed in nursery scenes, and this makeshift arrangement served well enough as a bassinet. But now the baby was five months old and too big to sleep in the egg carton anymore.

I was struggling through school while working nights, collecting and counting mosquitoes for the City Health Department in Jacksonville, Florida. If I'd been paid a penny for each mosquito in the traps, instead of by the hour, I could have afforded all sorts of luxuries, such as a crib for our third baby. But supporting a family of five on a part-time job imposes quite a few financial limitations, so the baby slept in the egg carton.

One night in family devotions, my wife explained the whole situation to our Lord. "Dear Jesus," Ginny prayed, "we've just got to have a new crib mattress. Eve is too big for her little box, and she needs a bed. You know we have that old crib in the storeroom, but it was secondhand when we got it. And after Jennifer and Donald outgrew it, that mattress was in tatters; so we need a new mattress. Soon, please. Amen."

Ginny's prayers made me mad. I felt frustrated because I was trying to live as I thought God wanted, and I felt he had let me down. I attended school because I thought he wanted me there. My job seemed to be the place he had for me, and I was trying to raise my family right. But I couldn't even afford a mattress for a secondhand baby crib. It just didn't seem fair.

Another thing complicated our situation. Early in our marriage Ginny and I had decided to attempt to live without buying anything on credit, without ever borrowing money and without ever telling anyone except God about our needs. We have not always stayed within these guidelines, but they represent part of a standard of faith we acknowledge. I suspect the real reason we first aspired to this lifestyle was that we were too hardheaded, proud, and stubborn to admit how poor we actually were. At any rate, the baby slept in a box, Ginny prayed, and I was mad at God.

One afternoon during the week after Ginny's prayer, one of my fellow students needed a ride to work after school, so I gave him a lift. We had to cross the Main Street Bridge over the St. Johns River. This bridge spans nearly a mile of river and is about a hundred feet above the water. It carries traffic for U.S. Highways 1 and 17 and is one of the most heavily traveled bridges in the city. A huge metal grating in the center of the bridge rises to allow ships to pass underneath in the main channel of the river. As we drove across that metal grating, something lay right in the center of the roadway—it looked like a brand-new crib mattress.

Since a truck was following me closely, I couldn't stop to check. I had to follow the flow of traffic into downtown Jacksonville, where one-way streets forced me to make an eight-block loop before I could head north over the bridge again. All this maneuvering took close to thirty minutes, but when I returned, incredibly, the crib mattress still lay on the grate, untouched by the busy traffic. Right then and there, I stopped being mad at the Lord.

I paused on the center span. My friend leaped out, threw the crib mattress in the backseat, and jumped in the car again as traffic honked behind us. The mattress probably had fallen from the back of a truck or something, and there was no way for me to locate its original owner. Except for a scuffed place at one corner, it appeared to be in perfect condition.

That night as Ginny and I put together our old crib to receive its new mattress, I hesitated. "Suppose it's not the right size for our crib?"

"Hand me the screwdriver," Ginny replied. "God wouldn't send us a mattress that doesn't fit."

She was right.

THE DRIVER

Lynn Erice

*T*here was a storm on its way that December night some years ago, but I didn't know it. Warnings were flashed on TV screens all across the state, but I didn't see them. The radio said not to leave your house unless you absolutely had to, but I didn't hear it. That night I was sitting in my apartment in Rochester, reading, and feeling overwhelmed. I had an impulsive urge to get away, and the farm seemed the only place I could go. Feeling lonesome for my mother, I said to Mealie, my dog, "Come on, let's go see Grandma."

Wearing just the clothes I had on, but no hat or boots, I walked out the door with Mealie at my heels. We climbed into my Datsun and headed toward Lyndonville, New York, where I had grown up. I'd left home when I was nineteen. I'd married and lived all over the United States, but always I'd returned. The farm reminded me of the stability I longed for, the security I'd lost.

After a bad marriage, I thought I'd finally made peace with living alone. I had a nice apartment and a steady job waiting tables, but I was lonely and unsure of the future. I'd always thought God had meant me to do more with my life. At thirty-six, I still felt that I hadn't accomplished anything.

The snow was coming down fast as I drove north through Rochester on Interstate 390, heading toward the Lake Ontario State Parkway. That was the most direct route west to Lyndonville, and I could avoid the traffic on the other roads.

There was a problem, though, when I reached the parkway. It hadn't been touched by snowplows, and the snow was already inches deep. I turned around at the first exit and drove back to Route 104, a much-traveled, well-maintained highway eight miles south.

"Guess I should have gone this way from the beginning," I told Mealie. "Now we're already twenty miles out of our way."

The snow on 104 looked bad too, but I didn't want to turn back. And I didn't want to admit I was scared. Mealie and I pushed on, driving very slowly, following the red taillights of the car ahead. The wind howled around us and the snow swirled so fiercely that I could see nothing else but those red taillights. It seemed pointless to turn back. After all, the weather would be just as bad going east as it was going west, and I wouldn't have any taillights to follow. In two hours of driving, not a vehicle had passed me going in the opposite direction.

Suddenly the red taillights stopped. A man stepped out and fought against the wind. As I rolled down my window to talk to him, the wind gushed in so hard that I could barely breathe.

He leaned down to me, "I'm stopping," he said. "I can't see anything at all now."

"Where are we?"

"Somewhere near Albion."

Albion! I had been driving two hours and was only as far as Albion! That's usually only a thirty-five-minute trip.

Trying to sound calm, I said, "I guess I'll keep going. There's no sense for me to stop here, I'm only going to Lyndonville."

"Okay," he said. "Good luck."

Within moments of leaving him, I had second thoughts. It was obvious that we had been the only two cars on the road. Now I was alone. Maybe I should go back, but why? I only had fifteen more miles to go.

I drove on. I was traveling alone in a vast expanse of whiteness, a sort of no-man's-land. The only way I stayed on course was by making out the mailboxes along the road. Now and again I veered toward one, and shaking with fear, I'd have to stop and maneuver my way onto the road again. Sometimes a glimpse of light beckoned from a faraway house. I was tempted to stop and try to make it on foot to the light. But wearing only jeans, a sweater, and sneakers, I was not prepared for a difficult walk through a blizzard. And if I stopped the car and stayed in it, the snow was coming down so fast that we would soon be buried under it.

Minute by minute, second by second, my mind raced along. My hands ached, locked around the steering wheel in a vicelike grip of fear and concentration. My body was so tense that it felt as though it were ready to break into pieces.

Now most of the windshield was covered with ice. The buildup on the wiper blades was so great that their rubber surfaces couldn't even make contact with the glass. Visibility was so poor that everything looked the same—a surreal landscape of stark white.

I could only inch forward. Suddenly the car jolted to a stop and in the split second it took for me to realize that I'd plowed into a snowbank, I screamed. Frantic, wild with fear, I began to argue with myself. "You fool, now you've done it. You'll never get out."

Calmly, something inside me said, *Just back out slowly. Drive out the way you came in.*

"No, you're stuck. You'll stay here and freeze to death. Mom won't even find out for days. Poor Mealie. She's afraid."

Back out slowly. It can be done.

Finally I took my mind's advice. Trying to calm Mealie in the seat beside me, I backed out slowly. My body sagged with relief. I straightened the car out and we started moving forward again. But what was the use? I peered desperately out the windshield. There was nothing but snow. No road, no lights, no mailboxes, just snow.

Shaking my head in disbelief, my eyes flooding with tears, I cried out, "Lord, help me. Please, Lord, I can't drive anymore. I can't go on. Take over. Please, Lord, drive this car for me."

No sooner were those words out of my mouth than something wondrous began to happen. Ahead, where moments before all had been white, a tiny spot of clear highway shone in my headlights. I drove toward it and then there was another. To my astonishment we kept moving forward, foot by foot, yard by yard.

"Thank you, Jesus," I prayed. In my desperation I had called out to him, and he answered. He was with me in the blizzard. Wouldn't he be with me always?

I drove on—or should I say the Lord drove. I sat in the driver's seat with my hands on the wheel, but I knew I wasn't driving. Gradually my courage returned and my tears disappeared. He was showing me I wasn't alone. I never had been.

Suddenly a set of tire tracks appeared from nowhere. I followed them until I was only three miles from the farm. At that point, after almost three and a half hours of driving, I finally saw a snowplow coming toward me in the opposite direction. Passing it, I switched lanes, taking advantage of the road it had cleared.

When at last I made it to the farm, Mealie jumped out of the car, and we both hurried into the warmth of the house. But now I felt secure. Like the psalmist, I knew for a fact that the Lord is my shepherd. He had brought me home.

THE BOLT IN THE ASPHALT

Stephanie Burt

Last summer I went with my church youth group on a mission trip to the Bahamas, where twice a day we performed a puppet show for youngsters in parks and schools. And twice a day, it seemed, our old school bus broke down.

One hot afternoon we were on our way to a performance when the bus came to a sudden halt. "Not again," everyone grumbled. Our youth leaders, Bill and Daryl, stepped out to see what was wrong.

Up until then I had maintained a good attitude about the bus's unreliability, but this was the last straw. We were stuck on a deserted side street in the sweltering heat with not even a phone booth nearby to call someone for help.

"Guys," Daryl reported, "this is serious. Our clutch

has broken and the bolt that holds it together has fallen off somewhere back on the road. We have a big bucket of spare nuts and bolts, but not one of them fits. Just pray."

We joined hands and fervently asked God for help. When we looked up, we saw an odd sight. Bill was kneeling on the pavement, picking something out of the asphalt with his pocketknife. He leaned under the hood of the bus with the object, then came to us with a big smile on his face.

"As you were praying, I looked down and there beside the tire, embedded in the pavement, was an old bolt. On an outside chance I dug it up and screwed it on. It fit!"

The bus started up again and we drove to the puppet show, filled with awe at the power of prayer.

FIVE

WHEN WE SEE CHRIST

*T*he Lord said to him in a vision, "Ananias."
He answered, "Here I am, Lord."

—Acts 9:10 NRSV

Jesus promised us that he would always be with us, and that he would send us a Comforter, just like himself, to be with us forever. So even though we do not see Jesus with our physical eyes, or in a vision, we trust him and his promise. Occasionally, however, the curtain is drawn back, and Jesus Christ shows himself to individuals. For some whose stories are included here, Jesus appeared to them in their desperate situations, to assure them they would ultimately be all right. To others, Jesus revealed himself in "ordinary" circumstances.

Though we ourselves may not receive a vision of Christ, all the stories in this volume call us to trust him, to give our lives to him, and to live in his presence.

THE INCREDIBLE RESCUE

Robert Bowden

I'm a carpenter, an ordinary man who works hard with his hands. I say this because the experience I'm going to tell you about is a strange one, and I want you to know I'm not the kind of man to go around making up outlandish stories.

That winter was a rough one for the building trades in Monmouth County, New Jersey, where my family lived. I write country and western music on the side and play the guitar and sing, so I was able to pick up a few jobs on weekends, but not enough to support my wife and three kids.

Then, just before Christmas, I landed my first solid job in months, on the nuclear power plant that was under construction at Salem, New Jersey, 129 miles from our home in Oakhurst. I was grateful for the work, even though it meant I had to live at a motel in Salem and go home to see my family only on weekends.

The nuclear plant was a massive project, involving over four thousand men. I was on the crew building the huge 250-foot cooling towers, like the ones at Three Mile Island in Pennsylvania. My particular job was to erect the wood platforms and the wooden forms—plywood sheets nailed to heavy frames—into which the concrete for the thick tower walls was poured.

All my working life I was used to heights, but climbing the steel to the tops of those towers, as high as a twenty-story building, made me nervous. On such a vast project there often are lots of injuries. Every day we heard stories of men losing fingers and toes, and even arms and legs.

One clear, sunny day in February, it was bitterly cold. I was glad I'd be working inside the tower, fairly close to the bottom, out of the wind, stripping the forms off the hardened walls.

Before I had been at the site ten minutes, the cold was numbing my fingers. High above, sunlight streamed through the circular mouth of the tower. Around me, in the freezing semi-twilight at the bottom, there was bedlam as the workers swarmed over the scaffolding. From the unfinished floors, a bristling bed of upright steel construction rods protruded.

I grabbed a hammer and a stripping crowbar and paused, looking up at the platform where I'd be working thirty-five feet above the floor.

"Hey, Jake!" I called to the foreman, my breath steaming the frigid air. "You only got one plank on that platform!"

"It's all right, Bob," he said, trotting over. "If we put up another plank, you won't have room to pull the forms away from the wall. Just be careful."

"Okay," I replied, but I was doubtful. An eight-inch-wide board isn't much to stand on.

I climbed up and began prying the forms loose. It was slow and hard, working so close to the wall on that shaky plank, and the plywood forms were heavy and awkward to handle.

By ten o'clock I had managed to get one off. I paused to warm my numbed hands. Down below, I could see my coworkers picking their way through the forest of upright steel rods. Nasty things. They were for reinforcing the floor; each one was five-eighths of an inch thick, and they varied in height from one to three feet. Their tips were flat. All the same, I had seen a fellow worker impaled on such rods about two years before. All it took was one careless move . . .

I began prying the second form loose. It wouldn't budge; it was stuck to the concrete. I pulled harder. Suddenly the crowbar slipped, throwing me off balance. I plunged forward toward the foot-wide opening where the other plank ordinarily would have been. I knew I was falling. Fear tore through me. I cried out, "God, help me!"

Then, incredibly, it happened. The wooden form and the gray wall of the tower vanished in a blaze of brilliant white light. In the middle of that beautiful, clear light, yet not part of it, stood a Man. He was dressed in a white robe made of some kind of silky cloth. There was a rope around his waist and sandals on his feet. His head was covered by a hood that appeared to be part of the robe. Framing the Man's face, and just visible under the hood, was dark brown, shoulder-length hair. He had a beard with a small part in the middle. His dark brown eyes were commanding but kindly.

Then he spoke. The voice was not in my head, but a real, external voice, beautiful and deep, and it seemed to echo. There is a verse in the Bible that reminds me of it: "And his voice was like the sound of many waters" (Revelation 1:15 NRSV).

As long as I live, I will never forget his words: "Son, I am going to save you. Just trust in me. Don't fight me."

Then he vanished. And I was falling, plunging facedown toward those upright steel rods, each one a dagger.

Strangely, all fear had left me. As my body hurtled down toward death, I thought: *Should I try to save myself somehow? Is there anything I can grab . . . ?* There was nothing.

Don't fight me, the Man's voice echoed through my mind. I abandoned myself to whatever might happen.

Suddenly, I felt some kind of Power turn my body. Now I was no longer falling facedown but sideways, rigidly, like a ruler on edge.

I slammed down between the steel rods. My back grazed the concrete floor, then I was jerked up as if on a giant string, bouncing crazily. Then everything was still.

Everybody came running. "Oh, my God! My God!" Jake kept saying.

"He landed on the rods—they're clean through him!" someone cried.

"I can't look! I'm gonna be sick!" somebody else said.

"No . . . no . . . I'm all right," I gasped. "Cut . . . my belt . . ."

A couple of guys rushed in to cut my belt. Suddenly I could breathe again.

"Good God!" Jake said, "I've never seen anything like this. How come those rods didn't go through him?"

My plummeting body had passed between the rods. The belt loop on my pants had snagged the tip of the tallest rod, about three feet above the floor. Miraculously, the loop held, breaking the force of my fall. Except for grazing my lower back on the concrete, I was suspended above the other rods.

Gently my co-workers lifted me off the rods and laid me on the floor. They gasped in shocked surprise when, a few seconds later, I stood up.

"I don't believe it!" one of the guys said. "He should be dead, but he's standing here!"

"Bob, the Lord was with you today," Jake said, "or this never could have happened."

"That's right, Jake," I said fervently, "the One who saved me was Jesus Christ. He gets the credit!" I was about to tell them what I had seen, but something stopped me. I figured they'd never believe me, in spite of the miracle they had just witnessed.

At the hospital, X rays revealed no broken bones. My only injury was a large bruise in my lower back, where it had hit the floor. The doctor prescribed muscle relaxants and sent me home.

The next morning, my coworker John, who also lived at the motel, was surprised to see me at breakfast.

"You're not going in today, old buddy, are you?" he asked.

"Sure," I replied, munching a piece of toast. "I'm okay."

"God was really with you yesterday, Bob," he said studying me.

I looked back at him, and decided to tell him the truth. "John, just as I fell off that scaffold I saw Jesus Christ."

He slowly lowered his cup and looked away. "That's impossible."

"No," I replied firmly, "It's not impossible. I saw him, and he saved my life." Then I told him about the vision.

"Bob," he said after I had finished, "It's not that I doubt your word . . . but I still think it's impossible. Still, you're here today, alive and healthy . . . so maybe it's not so impossible."

All that day I found myself wondering why the Lord had shown himself to me and had saved me. Why had I been singled out for a miracle? Did the Lord want me to do some great work in the world? How could I? I was just an ordinary workingman . . .

All of this happened quite a few years ago. I'm still a carpenter, and I still write songs and play and sing. If

God has a big job for me, it's still in the future, but I'm open to it. Meanwhile, I just try to be helpful and kind to troubled people whenever I meet them. That's something I can do right now—it's something we all can do.

Sometimes, when I think people will accept it, I tell them about the day when I saw Jesus and he saved my life. And their eyes light up with hope. They know that even if they can't see him, if he reached down and helped Bob Bowden out of a tight spot, then he'll surely help them, too. And I'm reminded of the words of Jesus himself: "Because thou hast seen me, thou hast believed: blessed are they that have not seen, and yet have believed" (John 20:29).

WHAT'S THE DOCTOR'S NAME?

Sam Nix

Here in South Korea, where I'm stationed with the U.S. military, I recently met Ms. Kyong Cha Lee, a woman who had suffered a terrible loss.

Ms. Lee's house, like many older homes in Korea, is heated by large charcoal briquettes placed under the floor. During a cold spell last spring this primitive heating system malfunctioned, spreading poisonous carbon monoxide fumes throughout the house, almost killing Ms. Lee.

She lay in the hospital in a coma for days, with her family at her bedside. When she finally awoke, they were too grieved to tell her the extent of her loss. But she astonished them when she said she already knew her two children had been killed in the tragedy. "The doctor told me when he came to look after me," she explained.

"What doctor?" they asked.

"The doctor who prayed by my side and promised that God would watch over me."

They assured her they had seen no such visitor and they had been with her constantly. The physician must have been a dream, they said.

When Ms. Lee was well enough to go home, she was making her way out of the hospital when she caught sight of a portrait in the lobby. "There," she said, "that's the doctor who came to my bedside. What is his name?" "Jesus Christ," came the answer.

And that's the story I heard from Ms. Lee at a retreat recently. She was there with a number of others who, like her, were new in the Christian faith.

THE LONER

Susan Peoples

The shadows in the canyon were already deepening to purple by the time my friend, David, and I left the biting cold of the mountain river to climb back up the ridge to the mesa above, where we'd stashed our heavy hiking gear. Wearing only

T-shirts and jeans, we had earlier descended a gentler slope to one side, drawn by the sight of that idyllic valley so far below. Now, looking up from the dusky canyon floor toward the looming cliff face, still rimmed at the top in gold from the rays of the setting sun, we decided to avoid the easier path and to climb straight up into the light.

The challenge suited me. I was proud of my strong, lean body—proud of my "toughness," my independence.

As we started the climb, I glanced toward David, whom I had met just a couple of weeks before. I had to admire his own lean strength as he nimbly scaled that rocky wall. I felt I could like him very much if I would choose to do so, but I'd fought against the idea—was still fighting it. Any kind of closeness to another human being seemed to me to be a dangerous thing. To invite a person to come near meant also to invite emotional pain, and *that* I could do without. I'd watched my parents suffer through a divorce when I'd been a child, and I hadn't liked what the stress did to them, or to me. I'd decided to keep everyone at a distance, to surround myself by an invisible wall. I would shut out all emotion and become totally self-sufficient.

I'd succeeded in that goal. After growing up and leaving home, I'd held several different jobs, one of them as manager of a restaurant. That, too, had been a challenge, but I'd liked being in charge of a business. Just as I liked being in charge of my own life and destiny, climbing up this cliff.

As the way grew steeper, edging toward vertical, I constantly tested the stability of the rocks before trusting them with my weight. Several times I found a rock to be loose and I searched for a different handhold or foothold before moving higher. Soon I had ascended almost two hundred feet. I glanced again toward David, seeing that he was off to one side and a little higher than I. We had only thirty or so more feet to go before reaching the top.

And then it happened. I hooked my fingers around the edge of a shelf of rock above me that I'd thought was secure, only to have it suddenly give way. With a feeling of disbelief, as though everything had gone into slow motion, I lost my balance and dropped into space, followed by a huge chunk of ledge. I heard David scream, "My God, O my God!"

God was someone else I'd shut out of my life. All my growing years I had attended a strict religious school where the teachers described God as an angry, vengeful being who would send me to hell for my sins. I didn't like that God, and I'd decided I wanted no part of him. I'd go it alone, assuming responsibility for my own actions, instead of cowering in fear before some cruel, mythical judge.

And so, even in my present extremity, falling toward death, I did not call on God. But David continued to cry out, not in prayer, but in an agonized, involuntary repetition of the name.

Now occurred in sequence several events so incredible that I find them hard to believe to this day. I had fallen with my face toward the cliff, but now *my body flipped around in midair,* like a cat's so that I was facing outward. Consequently, when my feet twice touched slight protrusions in the cliff's surface, I was tilted backward, toward the cliff face, instead of being catapulted farther into space. Then my feet landed on a small ledge, barely wide enough for one person, and the *only ledge on that whole cliff between me and the ground.* A few inches to either side, and I would have fallen past it. Sliding *between* two large cacti, I came to a halt with my legs hanging over the ledge. In one more second, I should have been crushed by the falling shelf of rock, which was several cubic feet in size. Instead, just before it would have hit me, it *veered inexplicably to the right,* grazing my shoulder and arm as it roared past.

I hung there in a daze, clutching at my narrow perch with my left hand while watching that boulder fall away toward the canyon floor one hundred fifty feet below. David came scrambling back down the cliff, frantically calling out to me. As he drew near, I heard him breathe, "Thank God, you're alive!" And then his voice changed as he groaned, "Susan—your leg . . . ."

As yet, I felt no pain. Consequently, it was with amazement that I viewed my shattered left leg. Through the tattered remnants of my jeans, I saw three holes in the flesh of my lower leg from which broken bones protruded. My foot hung twisted around at an odd angle, like the leg of a discarded doll. I turned my head away, only to see that the inside of my right arm had been sliced completely open, elbow to wrist, exposing ripped ligaments and tendons, and a rubbery length of artery— scratched but not severed—pulsing deep inside the gaping wound.

I looked back toward David and saw that he had turned dead-white. He asked me if I thought my spine was damaged. I took mental inventory of my body, trying to determine if I had internal injuries, but I just couldn't tell. At last David said, "I don't dare try to get you off this cliff alone. I'm going to have to leave you and go for help."

I knew he was right. But the initial shock that had numbed me was beginning to wear off. I was suddenly hit by pain so devastating it froze my breath.

"Hurry—just hurry," I gasped.

He scrambled away at an angle up the ridge, heading

toward the mesa and the trail that would take him out of these rugged Sangre de Cristo mountains (a Spanish name meaning "Blood of Christ") toward the jeep road, far away, where we'd left our four-wheel drive pickup truck. I knew that the nearest hospital had to be in Española, New Mexico, about twenty miles away. I also knew it would take hours for a rescue crew to hike in with a litter. The light faded fast, taking with it the last heat from the sun. I began to shiver in my thin shirt, for September nights in the high country get very cold. In the distance I heard the rumbling thunder of an approaching storm.

As the minutes passed, the pain grew in intensity until I felt consumed by it. The storm arrived, bringing darkness and an icy rain. The surface of the ledge became slick with water and mud, so that I had to concentrate all my strength in my left arm, trying to hold on.

My mind whirled with giddiness. It would be so easy to let go and slip into that void. To die, and end the pain.

I'd recently read a book called *Life After Life* in which people who had been declared clinically dead returned to life with stories about having met a sentient light filled with love. I didn't know if such a being existed. But if it did, it couldn't be that hateful personage called "God."

I wanted to pray to that light, but I didn't know what to call it. Finally, I did call it God, for want of a better name. I prayed for help to arrive, and for the strength to hold on until then. I said I was frightened. I said I didn't want to be alone.

And he came.

I saw no light. I heard no voice. All I can tell you is that suddenly, beside me on that ledge, there was a

Presence. A Presence filled with warmth and love. I could feel strength pouring into me from that Presence, joining with, and energizing, my own fading will.

The thoughts in my mind were in my own voice, but they said, *Hold on. You can make it. You are not alone. Help will come.*

The comfort I felt in this Presence is indescribable. Whenever I would begin to fade out, something would snap me awake once more and I would discover just enough willpower left in me to pull away from the edge.

But I wanted more. I wanted the touch of a human hand. All these years, I had kept people away. Now, suspended in air on this cold cliff, crying out in pain with almost every breath, I longed desperately for someone to hold me, to talk to me, to distract me from the prison of agony my body had become.

Time flowed into a meaningless blur. And then, between my cries, I heard someone, faint and far away, calling my name. Peering down into the darkness, I saw a tiny light bobbing along the canyon floor.

I called to that light, and the light answered. I saw it veer toward me and proceed, slowly but surely, up the cliff. A face came into view over the side of the ledge, eerily white in the flashlight's glow.

It was a child. A boy about twelve or thirteen years old. I thought for a moment that I was hallucinating. But the boy scrambled up beside me on the slippery ledge. He carefully set the flashlight down in a depression in the rocks. And then he took a folded blanket from his shoulder and draped it over me, shielding me from the rain.

"Who are you?" I whispered.

"I'm Michael," he replied.

He was real. The touch of his small, dirt-roughened hands told me that. He explained that David, frantically looking for a phone, had shown up at the door of Michael's house, outside the canyon. But Mr. Browne, Michael's father, had no phone and was too ill to help any kind of rescue effort. After hastily telling the Brownes about the accident, David had rushed away, heading once more down the mountain in his search for help.

"I thought you might be cold," Michael said, "so I came to find you."

He said he'd ridden his dirt bike until the brush got too thick. Then he'd hiked on into the canyon, and at last he'd heard my cries.

He asked what he could do for me, and I suggested that he elevate my injured arm. Surprisingly, my wounds had clotted soon after the accident, so I was no longer bleeding profusely; but elevating the arm seemed to help ease the pain. However, as we shifted on the ledge, I once more slipped toward the edge. Michael quickly grabbed my shoulders and held on, stopping my fall. After he had maneuvered me back to relative safety, he continued to hang on to me, while assuring me that the rescuers would arrive soon. He made me talk in order to keep me awake. Each time I started to slide forward on the slick surface of the ledge, Michael tightened his hold, dragging me back again. He was so determined to save me that I am convinced, had I actually gone over the edge, he would not have released his hold, but would have fallen with me to his own death.

As my mind wandered, I got to thinking that Michael might be a guardian angel. But he chattered on, like any normal boy, telling me about his friends in the Española Junior High and asking me questions just to make sure I was still with him.

I had totally lost track of time. I know now that Michael held me on that ledge for over two hours before more lights appeared in the canyon—David, with a doctor and two paramedics.

The ordeal they went through for the next several hours getting me off the cliff is another story. All I can say is that there were many acts of heroism from them all as they climbed the slippery rocks, splinting my leg and arm, strapping me into a litter, lowering me on ropes to the canyon floor. Michael acted as messenger, relaying instructions from one rescuer to another. All this in cold, wet darkness.

As groggy as I was, I still realized their terrible danger, and my prayer changed: *Please, God, don't let one of them die on this cliff in helping me.*

Because of a head injury I hadn't even known about, the doctor was not able to give me painkillers. My screams, every time I was accidentally jostled, had to be unnerving for the men, but they didn't give up. Even though they were cold and exhausted, they carried me as carefully as they could over the rough canyon floor and up the slopes to the pickup truck, then drove me over rocky jeep trails to the road where the ambulance waited. Because of the seriousness of my injuries, the doctors in Española couldn't treat me, but sent me on to St. Vincent's Hospital in Santa Fe. At last, twelve hours after my fall, I went into surgery, where the doctors pieced my torn and broken body back together.

I awoke to find myself immobilized in heavy casts. Me, Ms. Independence, totally helpless and having to rely on others for everything—bedpans, baths, food, therapy. Dozens of flower arrangements and over a hundred cards arrived, soon filling my room. Friends and acquaintances flocked to see me, saying eagerly, "You've always been such a loner, Susan, holding us off. But at last we're going to get to do something for you!"

The God I met on that ledge was neither angry nor condemning. The God I met there was love. Love, flowing from an unseen Presence to give me strength; love, coming from David and the rescue team as they struggled to get me off the cliff; love from doctors, nurses, and old friends; and love from Michael, a child who sustained me during that lonely, painful night.

When that rock fell, so did the wall I'd built around myself to shut out that love. I will never be the same.

EASTER AFFIRMATION

Elizabeth Searle Lamb

Today
   the risen Christ
   is risen in my heart
   in radiant, joyous Eastertide.
All doubts
all fears . . .
   the stone has rolled them all aside
   and faith springs up, alive,
   to welcome Him
today.

THE PROMISE

Debbie Parvin

*I*t was a warm, hazy, Illinois morning, the first of July—I remember waking up tired. Not just a yawn-and-stretch-before-getting-up tired, but a deep-down, aching fatigue.

"I guess I haven't recovered from the recital yet," I told myself, thinking back to a studio dance recital my students had given two weeks earlier. And with three young children home for summer vacation, my choir practice, fellowship group at church . . . well, that was good reason to be a little weary.

I lay back down on the pillow. In college I had always been into everything—dancing, singing, campus choirs, clubs, always racing for some meeting. And now with a family, it was still go, go, go. *It'll always be this way,* I thought.

Reminding myself that I had three children who would be up soon—my husband, Chuck, was already at work—I climbed out of bed . . . and fell flat on my back. *What a klutz!* I thought, as I tried to get up but couldn't. I crawled slowly backward down the stairs to the living room, and hoisted myself onto the sofa.

Surely this won't last, I thought. But it did. The pain grew daily in intensity, sharp and piercing, jumping without any pattern from one part of my body to another. Muscle spasms locked my back in an arched position for hours on end. Finally, I had to be hospitalized.

Meanwhile, a team of doctors worked feverishly to discover what disease I had. Results of test after test were sent to many clinics, and for six agonizing months there was no answer. And then . . . "Dermatomyositis," my doctor told Chuck. "It will slowly destroy Debbie's muscles and vital organs. And we have no cure."

By now I couldn't sit up for more than a half hour at a time. I was too weak to lift a magazine or answer the telephone. As time went on, the doctor's words to my husband held no hope: "She'll be completely bedridden within two years, and probably won't live longer than five years." Period. I was a professional dancer who could no longer walk; a mother who no longer had the strength to raise her five-, seven-, and nine-year-old children.

I might have given up right there, if not for a very strange and wonderful thing that happened during that first hospital stay.

I was alone in my room, half asleep. Some friends from the church had stopped by earlier to visit. Chuck was at work, so I knew he wouldn't be in until later. That's why I was so surprised when I heard those words so distinctly, as if someone were talking to me. I opened my eyes, but there wasn't anyone else in the room—only those words, still ringing in my ears: "The joy of the Lord is your strength."

"Why, I recognize that," I said. "It's from Nehemiah, the tenth verse of the eighth chapter." And then I laughed. I had always believed in God and the Bible, but the one thing I had never been able to do was memorize specific verses, not even as a youngster in Sunday school classes. "The joy of the Lord is your strength. Nehemiah eight, ten." The words came again, clear and unmistakable. I had to find out.

When Chuck came in, I greeted him quickly. "You

must read a Bible verse to me. In Nehemiah, chapter eight, verse ten."

Chuck took my Bible off the night stand, flipped the pages to Nehemiah and said, "Well, it says, 'Then he said to them, "Go your way, eat. . ."' Why do you want me to read this?"

"Just keep reading, please."

"'"... and do not be grieved, for the joy of the Lord is your strength."' That's all there is."

I fought to sit up in bed a little. "Honey, you know I've never been able to memorize Bible verses, right?"

"Yes."

"Today I started repeating that verse, perfectly, in my mind. And I don't remember hearing it before. I think God has given me this verse as his promise, that his strength will always sustain me. This is God's promise that I will be healed."

And so began a journey of faith, buoyed by a verse that had been as unknown to me as the illness that had brought it to me.

After I was released from the hospital, Chuck asked for night duties at the Chicago newspaper where he worked, so he could stay with me during the day while the children were at school. We remodeled the house, putting as much as possible on one floor of our split-level so I could get around in my wheelchair. Friends and neighbors brought meals, did the laundry and housework, and offered prayers. I prayed for healing, too—and anticipated a miracle.

Although I was severely restricted, I continued to sing in the church choir for a while. As a form of therapy, my doctor allowed me to continue teaching dance, offering verbal rather than physical instructions. I sometimes taught while lying on a couch in my downstairs studio. I played games with our three children and gave them singing lessons. And all the while I remembered my promise: "The joy of the Lord is your strength."

But a healing, even a respite, didn't come. As weeks turned into months and then into years, I was progressively forced to give up even the simplest outside activities. Although there were days when I might walk fifty steps at one time, it was usually the exception rather than the rule. There was always pain; often hospitalization was the only way to control it. And as my health began to ebb away, so did that kinetic energy of living. The simplest of activities would sap all my strength.

Chuck had become both dad and mom, the breadwinner and the breadmaker. By noon, after soothing my anxieties, he was off to the local McDonald's, serving hamburgers to help meet our mounting medical bills. Then home to greet the children after school, before he and they fixed dinner. And after watching a favorite television show with the children and settling them into bed, it was off to be night editor at the *Tribune*.

The children had to adjust too, suddenly faced with responsibility beyond their years. There was no one to catch them in the cookie jar, sure; but there was also no mother to take them to Cub Scouts, to write out an algebra problem, to be waiting up for them after a night out. Usually all I could do was listen to them, and I did, too, every chance I got. I hung on every word of every story they told me, stories that before the illness I was too busy to hear. If I was strong enough to take thirty steps, twenty-seven were for the children—meeting them at the door after school, sharing breakfast. I loved them dearly, and needed them to know that.

I passed the five-year limit the doctor had set, the joy of being alive always tempered by the loneliness and frustration life meant. The only sure element in the uncertainty of disease, in the struggle to keep hope, was

Nehemiah—day and night I embraced those words as a small child does a favorite blanket or toy.

Church was my special treat—I insisted on going as often as I was able. "Please, Chuck," I remember pleading after one particularly bad week. "I *have* to be there."

Chuck agreed and, after wheeling me up the special ramp the church had built, helped me to my feet and took my arm in his. Ever so slowly we walked down the center aisle of the church—step, rest, another step or two. I always tried hard to smile, because it helped me forget the pain. About halfway down and five minutes later, Chuck guided me into a pew and helped support me during the service. It was a process we were to repeat many times. Together, I hoped, we could persevere.

Eight, nine, ten years passed—and the children started off to college. Chuck swapped hamburgers for high-school teaching, and I prayed. It was one thing I could do easily. Then, eleven years after that dreadful morning, my doctor gave up hope as the disease intensified.

"Debbie, I can't allow you to increase your medication. We've reached the absolute maximum limit. I'm sorry . . ." He paused. "There is nothing more I can do for you."

My muscles were so useless that most days I had difficulty turning over in bed. Chuck wore a brave face, but my insistence that healing would yet come rang hollow against my medical chart.

Then one night in November, as I lay in bed, I was praying. Suddenly I had a sensation of someone else being in the room.

I opened my eyes; and there, not five feet away, he stood—his long, bluish-white robe flowing, his arms outstretched toward me. There were no clearly distinguishable features about him, only a soft glow. I felt an indescribable blend of shock, amazement, reverence, awe. There was no doubt in my mind that I was seeing Jesus.

"You have been healed," he said in a very audible, very compassionate voice. He went on to tell me certain things. That I was not to stop using the wheelchair and the medication at once, only gradually. That he had given the doctors and researchers their abilities, and that to stop treatment immediately would be a defiance of that gift. Finally he told me not to tell anyone what had happened—not just yet. Then he was gone.

For a moment I just stared, but then, as naturally as taking a breath, I began to stand up. I had been on my knees, at the side of the bed, the entire time. I didn't know how I had gotten there, only that now I was standing. I hadn't been able to do that in ten years.

I walked—that was a miracle in itself—to my dressing room, where my medication was stored. Just as I had been told, I took a slightly reduced amount of my nightly dosage. At that point, I was taking more than three dozen pills a day.

It was difficult not to tell anyone—especially Chuck—but soon my drastic turnaround in health began speaking for itself. "I don't know what's happening," my doctor said during one of my routine examinations. "You were sinking so fast before, and now you seem to be getting better. I've never known of anyone with your disease to have a remission like this."

I felt the time had come. "Thanks to your efforts," I began cautiously, "and to God's healing power, it isn't a remission. I just don't have it anymore."

His look was incredulous. "Debbie, I don't believe that, and I can't accept it. I'm afraid this good spell is only temporary."

But future test results only affirmed my faith—there was no sign of dermatomyositis anywhere in my body. And my heart, damaged by the disease, now was perfect; an ulcer and hernia were also healed.

Just as Jesus had said that night, it took me more than a year and a half to free myself completely from the wheel-chair and medication. But since that time—for more than six years now—I have been free of the disease.

Was my meeting with Jesus just a dream, my healing a remission? Some still choose to believe that, and that is their choice. But the fact remains that once I was crippled, now I am whole. Once I couldn't walk, but now, by the grace of God, I can dance.

It was a long and difficult wait, thirteen years of pain and grief. I don't know why God chose to heal me when he did. But I do know that until he did, he sustained me and those around me with the strength and patience we needed to cope with those days and years of pain. And he still does today.

Truly, the joy of the Lord is my strength. In sickness and in health.

THE PAINTING

Bill Zdinak

I guess I was what you might call a lost soul—or something very close to it—when the telephone call came. It was from a member of a nearby church, and I remember how bored and impatient I felt as I listened to her. She knew that I was an artist, she said. She wanted to know if I would submit a painting for the church's annual art show, five months away.

In those days I took the line of least resistance about almost everything. If the show was almost half a year away, I figured I could worry about it later. In any case, it was easier to say yes than to say no. "Oh, sure," I told her. "I'll submit something." I hung up and promptly forgot all about it.

One reason I wasn't interested in the church member's call was that there was no money in it and, as usual, I was looking for the big deal. Two years earlier, what seemed like a very big deal had been right in my hands, and then had slipped through my fingers as the result of an incredible freak accident that almost took my life.

The deal had been a contract with a major automobile manufacturer to help promote a new car. It was all signed, and a lot of money was involved. To celebrate, I had agreed to go with some friends on a fishing trip to Canada. One morning, after a walk around the lake, I came back ready for a shower. Forgetting the warnings I'd had that the water was very hot, I stepped into the enclosed tub and shut the glass doors. In minutes the water turned to scalding steam. The glass door was stuck, and I couldn't slide it open. The pain was terrible. I began screaming at the top of my lungs. I couldn't reach forward to the handle for the water. My legs became numb, I couldn't see, and I had a terrifying fear that I would be blinded! That would mean the end of my career!

I started to fall, and my hand went through the glass. Suddenly I knew I had to hurl myself through the door to escape from that scalding prison. I covered my eyes and somersaulted through the glass. My head hit the opposite wall and I lay on the bathroom floor in a jumbled mass of shattered glass and blood.

My friends finally managed to get a doctor, who spent more than two hours stitching up my wounds. My life was saved, but during my period of recuperation, I discovered that I couldn't draw anymore. I had lost the use of my hands. The automobile manufacturer's project fell through. All my hopes and dreams had gone down the drain.

For anyone else, this experience might have been the time for some soul-searching and for a real reevaluation of goals and values, but I viewed my experience at that time only as a humiliating defeat. I felt that God had let me down, and I was bitter and resentful.

I found work as a consultant and was able to support my family, but I still measured success only in terms of money. That was unfortunate because, materially speaking, things went from bad to worse. Finally I lost my own studio, and a large New York firm offered to back me in a small shop. I wasn't particularly concerned about the integrity of the firm, and it turned out that they were dishonest. I was lucky to get out with only a minimal loss.

So here I was, back where I had started—still trying to make a lot of money fast, and still bombing. After two years, I regained about 75 percent use of my hands and was able to draw again, but things just didn't pick up for me. None of my deals panned out. I kept brooding about the lost contract and wondering why my life had got into such a mess. It was about that time I got the call from the church.

Five months can go by very quickly. One day the phone rang, and I heard a vaguely familiar voice saying, "Mr. Zdinak, we don't have your painting yet—the one for our annual exhibit."

I remembered then, all right.

In my usual manner I had promised everything and

fulfilled nothing. But even now a lie was easier than the truth. "I'm sorry," I said. "I don't have it quite finished yet." I was really disgusted with myself. Why hadn't I just told her I had forgotten it?

She asked me what size it was. Glancing around the room, I saw a frame with my wife's picture in it. So I gave her that size. "Fine," she said, "we'll save that space for you. But we really need it soon. Please don't let us down!"

I started then to contrive a religious picture. But nothing worked. By 2:00 A.M., twelve hours later, I had made a dozen worthless starts. Angry thoughts raged through my head. *I'm a phony and I'm so sick of living this way. My life is a mess. Everything is a mess. I can't make it on my own.* In complete frustration I cried out, "O God! This is what I get for lying! Please help me."

I threw down my brushes, and instantly there was a flash of light in the room. In that split second I saw on the canvas the image I was to paint. It was a head of Christ, but it was to be composed of many small faces —men, women, and children of all races and backgrounds, national and spiritual leaders as well as ordinary people. *That's it!* I thought, and hastily grabbed pictures of faces from around the studio. I began to paint in a way I had never known before. I did each face with rapid brush strokes and no preliminary sketches. Some unseen power guided my hand; I couldn't seem to make a false stroke. I knew something wonderful was happening, and I thought, *God, just let it continue.*

In fifteen hours all the faces had been finished. I stepped back to view the work and knew that it was the best thing I had ever done. Artists and art critics told me later that it was impossible for me to have done such a painting so quickly. I don't really understand

AQUINAS COLLEGE LIBRARY

35060001905556

what happened, but I do know that the painting is the best thing that ever happened in my life.

Over the years, it has continued to work its positive effect. Art shows continue to exhibit it. In each show it attracts crowds of viewers. People who have seen it tell me they've found it spiritually uplifting; in some cases it has inspired people to the extent that their lives have been changed.

I have refused to accept any profits from the painting because it isn't really my doing any more than my life is any longer my own life. It taught me an important lesson. Every time in the past when I tried to play all the angles and make the big money, something went wrong. Now my life is a success, and I give all the credit where it belongs—to God.

I have become deeply committed to working for Christ. Christ is in my life every day, not just on Sunday. I turn down advertising work if I feel it is selling something I can't morally approve. I try to accept only work that is pleasing to God. I begin my day and end my day thanking him. I never knew what success really meant until I gave myself up to him and let him be my guide. I find that he is with me just as he promised—always—and everywhere.